Target
Get back on track

GRADE 5

Edexcel GCSE (9-1)
English Language
Reading

David Grant

Pearson

Contents

 This workbook has been developed using the Pearson Progression Map and Scale for English.

To find out more about the Progression Scale for English and to see how it relates to indicative GCSE 9–1 grades go to www.pearsonschools.co.uk/ProgressionServices

Helping you to formulate grade predictions, apply interventions and track progress.

Any reference to indicative grades in the Pearson Target Workbooks and Pearson Progression Services is not to be used as an accurate indicator of how a student will be awarded a grade for their GCSE exams.

You have told us that mapping the Steps from the Pearson Progression Maps to indicative grades will make it simpler for you to accumulate the evidence to formulate your own grade predictions, apply any interventions and track student progress. We're really excited about this work and its potential for helping teachers and students. It is, however, important to understand that this mapping is for guidance only to support teachers' own predictions of progress and is not an accurate predictor of grades.

Our Pearson Progression Scale is criterion referenced. If a student can perform a task or demonstrate a skill, we say they are working at a certain Step according to the criteria. Teachers can mark assessments and issue results with reference to these criteria which do not depend on the wider cohort in any given year. For GCSE exams however, all Awarding Organisations set the grade boundaries with reference to the strength of the cohort in any given year. For more information about how this works please visit: https://qualifications.pearson.com/en/support/support-topics/results-certification/understanding-marks-and-grades.html/Teacher

① Tackling an unseen text

This unit will help you tackle the unseen texts which you will encounter in your exams. The skills you will build are to:

- check your reading skills have allowed you to understand the text
- identify the key ideas or points the writer wants to get across to the reader
- identify the writer's intention.

In the exam you will face questions like the ones below. These are about the text on page 2. This unit will prepare you to write your own response to questions like these – and help you prepare to answer the other questions on your exams.

Exam-style question

From lines 20–26, identify **one** phrase which shows that Mr Squeers cannot understand why no parents have come to the coffee house to send their sons to his school.　**(1 mark)**

Exam-style question

From lines 1–10, identify **two** phrases which suggest something about Mr Squeers' personality. You may use your own words or quotation from the text.　**(2 marks)**

The three key questions in the **skills boosts** will help you tackle an unseen text.

① How can I make sure I have understood the text?

② How do I identify the key ideas in the text?

③ How do I identify the writer's intentions?

Read the extract on page 2 from *Nicholas Nickleby* by Charles Dickens, first published in the 1830s. You will tackle a 19th century fiction extract in the Reading section of your Paper 1 exam.

As you read, remember the following: ✓

Before reading the extract, carefully read any introduction provided. It is intended to help you understand where the text is taken from, why it was written and other useful background information you might need.

While reading the extract, if you lose understanding of the text, stop and re-read from the last sentence or paragraph that you clearly understood.

After reading the extract, read it again.

In this extract, Mr Wackford Squeers, the headmaster of Dotheboys Hall, is waiting in a London coffee shop to meet any parents who might want to send their sons to his school.

Text 1 Nicholas Nickleby, Charles Dickens

He had but one eye, and the popular prejudice runs in favour of two. The eye he had, was unquestionably useful, but decidedly not ornamental: being of a greenish grey, and in shape resembling the fan-light of a street door. The blank side of his face was much wrinkled and puckered up, which gave him a very sinister appearance, especially when he smiled, at which times his expression bordered closely on the villainous. His hair was very flat and shiny,

5 save at the ends, where it was brushed stiffly up from a low protruding forehead, which assorted well with his harsh voice and coarse manner. He was about two or three and fifty, and a trifle below the middle size; he wore a white neckerchief with long ends, and a suit of scholastic black; but his coat sleeves being a great deal too long, and his trousers a great deal too short, he appeared ill at ease in his clothes, and as if he were in a perpetual state of astonishment at finding himself so respectable.

10 Mr. Squeers was standing in a box by one of the coffee-room fire-places, fitted with one such table as is usually seen in coffee-rooms, and two of extraordinary shapes and dimensions made to suit the angles of the partition. In a corner of the seat, was a very small deal trunk, tied round with a scanty piece of cord; and on the trunk was perched—his lace-up half-boots and corduroy trousers dangling in the air—a diminutive boy, with his shoulders drawn up to his ears, and his hands planted on his knees, who glanced timidly at the schoolmaster, from time to

15 time, with evident dread and apprehension.

'Half-past three,' muttered Mr. Squeers, turning from the window, and looking sulkily at the coffee-room clock. 'There will be nobody here today.'

Much vexed by this reflection, Mr. Squeers looked at the little boy to see whether he was doing anything he could beat him for. As he happened not to be doing anything at all, he merely boxed his ears, and told him not to do it

20 again.

'At Midsummer,' muttered Mr. Squeers, resuming his complaint, 'I took down ten boys; ten twenties is two hundred pound. I go back at eight o'clock tomorrow morning, and have got only three—three oughts is an ought—three twos is six—sixty pound. What's come of all the boys? What's parents got in their heads? What does it all mean?'

Here the little boy on the top of the trunk gave a violent sneeze.

25 'Halloa, sir!' growled the schoolmaster, turning round. 'What's that, sir?'

'Nothing, please sir,' replied the little boy.

'Nothing, sir!' exclaimed Mr. Squeers.

'Please sir, I sneezed,' rejoined the boy, trembling till the little trunk shook under him.

'Oh! Sneezed, did you?' retorted Mr. Squeers. 'Then what did you say "nothing" for, sir?'

30 In default of a better answer to this question, the little boy screwed a couple of knuckles into each of his eyes and began to cry, wherefore Mr Squeers knocked him off the trunk with a blow on one side of the face, and knocked him on again with a blow on the other.

'Wait till I get you down into Yorkshire, my young gentleman,' said Mr Squeers, 'and then I'll give you the rest. Will you hold that noise, sir?'

35 'Ye—ye—yes,' sobbed the little boy, rubbing his face very hard with the Beggar's Petition in printed calico.

'Then do so at once, sir,' said Squeers. 'Do you hear?'

How can I make sure I have understood the text?

It can be tempting to hope that you will fully understand an unseen text once you start answering the questions about it. This page will help you develop strategies to make sure you fully understand the text **before** you answer the questions!

1. When you read a new text, you may come across an unfamiliar word or phrase.
You can **either** try to work out its meaning using the rest of the sentence to help you **or** ignore it (if it's not affecting your understanding of the rest of the text).

   a. Look at some of the more unusual words and phrases from the extract on page 2. Look closely at the sentence in which each appears. Note down what each word or phrase might mean.

   i. fan-light (line 2) ....

   ii. trifle (line 6) ....

   iii. neckerchief (line 7) ....

   iv. scholastic (line 7) ....

   v. the Beggar's Petition in printed calico (line 35) ....

   b. Which of the words and phrases above do you think you could ignore without affecting your understanding of the rest of the text? Mark them with an ⊗.

2. When you have read an unseen text once or twice, you should be able to answer these questions:

   A. What kind of text is it? Fiction or non-fiction?

   B. What's the text about? Can you sum it up in five words or fewer?

   C. What's the purpose of the text? To inform, to describe, to argue, or something else?

   D. Why do you think the writer decided to write it?

   E. Does the writer clearly express or hint at their opinion about the ideas, characters or events in the text? What do you think their opinion is?

Write two or three sentences about the extract. Make sure that your sentences answer the questions above. Underline Ⓐ and label your writing to show where in your sentences you have answered questions A–E.

....

....

....

....

....

....

....

How do I identify the key ideas in the text?

Identifying the main ideas in a text helps you to:
- improve your understanding of the text as a whole
- explore how and why the text was written.

(1) One way to gather the main ideas in a text is to identify the key idea(s) in each paragraph or section of text. You are going to write a summary of each section of the text on page 2 **using ten words or fewer**. Carefully read:
- the first paragraph (lines 1–9)
- the second paragraph (lines 10–15)
- paragraphs three to five (lines 16–24)
- paragraph six to the end of the extract (lines 25–36).

When you have read each section, answer the questions in the table below, circling (A) Yes or No.

Write your summary of each paragraph below when you are happy that you have understood its main idea(s).

Paragraph:	1	2	3–5	6–end
Does the **first** sentence sum up the main point of this section?	Yes / No	Yes / No	Yes / No	Yes / No
Does the **last** sentence sum up the main point of this section?	Yes / No	Yes / No	Yes / No	Yes / No
Can you make any connection between the pieces of information in this section which would effectively sum up its main idea(s)?	Yes / No	Yes / No	Yes / No	Yes / No

Paragraph 1:..

....

Paragraph 2:..

....

Paragraph 3–5: ....

....

Paragraph 6–end: ....

....

(2) Now that you have identified the key ideas in the text on page 2, you should be able to locate the answers to the questions below quickly and easily.

Exam-style question

From lines 20–26, identify **one** phrase which shows the boy's attitude to Mr Squeers. **(1 mark)**

....

Exam-style question

From lines 1–10 identify **two** phrases which suggest that Mr Squeers is in a bad mood. **(2 marks)**

....

....

3 How do I identify the writer's intentions?

Your understanding of the writer's intentions in a text will guide and support your responses to **all** the questions in the exam.

1 Writers always have an **intention** when they write a text. This could be to influence the reader's:
   - actions – to persuade the reader to go and do something
   - ideas – to develop the reader's understanding or influence their opinion
   - emotions – to make the reader feel a particular way about an idea, event or person.

   Write 🖉 a sentence summing up what you think the writer's intention might be in the extract on page 2.

   ....

   ....

   ....

   ....

2 One way to help you understand the writer's purpose and intention is to consider whether there is evidence of **bias** in the text. Look at these sentences from the extract on page 2.

   > In default of a better answer to this question, the little boy screwed a couple of knuckles into each of his eyes and began to cry, wherefore Mr Squeers knocked him off the trunk with a blow on one side of the face, and knocked him on again with a blow on the other.

   a Can you identify ✓ any element of these sentences which reveals the writer's bias? Are they trying to influence your response to:

	Yes	No
Squeers?		
The boy?		

   b If you answered 'Yes' to Squeers or the boy, what impact do you think the writer wants his opinion to have on the reader? If you answered 'No', why do you think the writer might want the text to appear unbiased? 🖉

   ....

   ....

   ....

   ....

   c Look again at the whole extract on page 2. Underline Ⓐ any evidence which suggests that the writer is either biased or unbiased. Annotate 🖉 any evidence you underline, noting the impact it might have on the reader.

Extracting details from an unseen text

Some of the questions you will face in your exams are designed to test your skill in extracting information from an unseen text. Once you have read and understood the text fully, and identified the writer's main points, you are ready to tackle these kinds of question.

Look at one student's answers to the exam-style question below and their reasons for choosing them in the thought bubbles below.

Exam-style question

From lines 18–26, give **two** ways in which the writer suggests that Mr Squeers is not a good headmaster.

(2 marks)

Lines 18–26

'Half-past three,' muttered Mr. Squeers, turning from the window, and looking sulkily at the coffee-room clock. 'There will be nobody here today.'

20   Much vexed by this reflection, Mr. Squeers looked at the little boy to see whether he was doing anything he could beat him for. As he happened not to be doing anything at all, he merely boxed his ears, and told him not to do it again.

'At Midsummer,' muttered Mr. Squeers, resuming his complaint, 'I took down ten boys; ten twenties is two hundred pound. I go back at eight o'clock tomorrow morning, and have got only three—three oughts is

25   an ought—three twos is six—sixty pound. What's come of all the boys? What's parents got in their heads? What does it all mean?'

? Both of these suggest to me that Squeers is bad-tempered because no one has come to see him.

? The writer is presenting him here as violent and cruel to the boy.

? This makes me think he just thinks of his pupils as a way to make money.

Do you agree with the student's thoughts? Write 🖉 a sentence or two to explain your ideas.

....

....

....

....

....

....

....

....

Your turn!

After you have read and understood the text, identified its key points and explored the writer's intention, you are ready to tackle **all of the questions** you are likely to be asked in your exam.

Test your knowledge with the exam-style questions below.

Lines 1–10

He had but one eye, and the popular prejudice runs in favour of two. The eye he had, was unquestionably useful, but decidedly not ornamental: being of a greenish grey, and in shape resembling the fan-light of a street door. The blank side of his face was much wrinkled and puckered up, which gave him a very sinister appearance, especially when he smiled, at which times his expression bordered closely on the villainous.

5 His hair was very flat and shiny, save at the ends, where it was brushed stiffly up from a low protruding forehead, which assorted well with his harsh voice and coarse manner. He was about two or three and fifty, and a trifle below the middle size; he wore a white neckerchief with long ends, and a suit of scholastic black; but his coat sleeves being a great deal too long, and his trousers a great deal too short, he appeared ill at ease in his clothes, and as if he were in a perpetual state of astonishment at finding himself so

10 respectable.

Lines 20–26

20 Much vexed by this reflection, Mr. Squeers looked at the little boy to see whether he was doing anything he could beat him for. As he happened not to be doing anything at all, he merely boxed his ears, and told him not to do it again.

'At Midsummer,' muttered Mr. Squeers, resuming his complaint, 'I took down ten boys; ten twenties is two hundred pound. I go back at eight o'clock tomorrow morning, and have got only three—three oughts is

25 an ought—three twos is six—sixty pound. What's come of all the boys? What's parents got in their heads? What does it all mean?

Exam-style question

(1) From lines 20–26, identify **one** phrase which shows that Mr Squeers cannot understand why no parents have come to the coffee house to send their sons to his school. **(1 mark)**

....

....

(2) From lines 1–10, identify **two** phrases which suggest something about Mr Squeers' personality. **(2 marks)**

....

....

....

....

Review your skills

Check up

Review your response to the exam-style question on page 7. Tick ✓ the column to show how well you think you have done each of the following.

	Not quite ✓	Nearly there ✓	Got it! ✓
understood the text	☐	☐	☐
identified the key ideas in the text	☐	☐	☐
identified the writer's intention	☐	☐	☐

Look over all of your work in this unit. Note down 🖉 the three most important things to remember when you first read an unseen text.

1. ....

2. ....

3. ....

Need more practice?

Here is another exam-style question, this time relating to Text 2 on page 74: an extract from *I Know Why the Caged Bird Sings* by Maya Angelou. You'll find some suggested points to refer to in the Answers section.

Exam-style question

① From lines 1–5, identify **one** reason that the writer is worried about her brother. (1 mark)

....

② From lines 15–28, give **two** examples that suggest Bailey is unhappy. (2 marks)

....

....

How confident do you feel about each of these **skills?** Colour 🖉 in the bars.

❶ How can I make sure I have understood the text?

❷ How do I identify the key ideas in the text?

❸ How do I identify the writer's intentions?

Select and synthesise evidence (AO1)
Explain, comment on and analyse how writers use language and structure to achieve effects and influence readers (AO2)

② Analysing a text

This unit will help you analyse a text, a skill you will need to demonstrate in **all** the longer answers you have to write in your exams. The skills you will build are to:

- select relevant points to make in your analysis
- support your analysis with evidence
- develop your analysis.

In the exam you will face questions like the one below. This is about the text on page 10. At the end of the unit you will write your own response to this question.

Exam-style question

Analyse how the writer uses language and structure to interest and engage readers.

Support your views with detailed reference to the text.

(15 marks)

The three key questions in the **skills boosts** will help you analyse the text.

① How do I begin to analyse a text?

② How do I select quotations?

③ How do I develop my analysis?

Read the extract on page 10 from a newspaper article, written in 1940. You will tackle a 20th century non-fiction extract in the Reading section of your Paper 2 exam.

As you read, remember the following: ✓

Remember the focus of the exam question you are preparing to respond to.

Think about the ways in which the writer tries to interest and engage readers.

Underline Ⓐ or tick ✓ any parts of the text that **you** find engaging or interesting.

In 1940 during World War II, Hitler began to bomb London in an attempt to demoralise the British people. This period of relentless, heavy bombing became known as 'the Blitz'. Ernie Pyle was an American War Correspondent who died in Japan in 1945.

Text 1 The Blitz, Ernie Pyle

It was a night when London was ringed and stabbed with fire.

They came just after dark, and somehow you could sense from the quick, bitter firing of the guns that there was to be no monkey business this night.

Shortly after the sirens wailed you could hear the Germans grinding overhead. In my room, with its **black curtains**
5   drawn across the windows, you could feel the shake from the guns. You could hear the boom, crump, crump, crump, of heavy bombs at their work of tearing buildings apart. They were not too far away.

Half an hour after the firing started I gathered a couple of friends and went to a high, darkened balcony that gave us a view of a third of the entire circle of London. As we stepped out onto the balcony a vast inner excitement came over all of us – an excitement that had neither fear nor horror in it, because it was too full of awe.

10   You have all seen big fires, but I doubt if you have ever seen the whole horizon of a city lined with great fires – scores of them, perhaps hundreds.

There was something inspiring just in the awful savagery of it.

The closest fires were near enough for us to hear the crackling flames and the yells of firemen. Little fires grew into big ones even as we watched. Big ones died down under the firemen's valour, only to break out again later.

15   About every two minutes a new wave of planes would be over. The motors seemed to grind rather than roar, and to have an angry pulsation, like a bee buzzing in blind fury.

The guns did not make a constant overwhelming din as in **those terrible days of September**. They were intermittent – sometimes a few seconds apart, sometimes a minute or more. Their sound was sharp, nearby; and soft and muffled, far away. They were everywhere over London.

20   Into the dark shadowed spaces below us, while we watched, whole batches of **incendiary bombs** fell. We saw two dozen go off in two seconds. They flashed terrifically, then quickly simmered down to pin points of dazzling white, burning ferociously. These white pin points would go out one by one, as the unseen heroes of the moment smothered them with sand. But also, while we watched, other pin points would burn on, and soon a yellow flame would leap up from the white centre. They had done their work – another building was on fire.

25   Later on I borrowed a tin hat and went out among the fires. That was exciting too; but the thing I shall always remember above all the other things in my life is the monstrous loveliness of that one single view of London on a holiday night – London stabbed with great fires, shaken by explosions, its dark regions along the Thames sparkling with the pin points of white-hot bombs, all of it roofed over with a ceiling of pink that held bursting shells, **balloons**, flares and the grind of vicious engines. And in yourself the excitement and anticipation and wonder in
30   your soul that this could be happening at all.

These things all went together to make the most hateful, most beautiful single scene I have ever known.

black curtains: all windows and doors had to be covered to stop any light helping enemy aircraft to identify possible targets
those terrible days of September: the Blitz began in September 1940
incendiary bombs: bombs designed to start fires
balloons: huge, tethered balloons were floated above London to deter low-flying aircraft

How do I begin to analyse a text?

When you begin to analyse a text, you need to identify those parts of the text which will help you to respond to the question you are answering. When you have done that, you can begin to select quotations to support your choices.

Look again at the exam-style question you are exploring:

Exam-style question

Analyse how the writer uses language and structure to <u>interest and engage</u> readers.

(1) Which of these sections of the text do **you** find most <u>engaging and interesting</u>? Give each one a mark between 0 and 5.

	Section	✎	✓
A.	The first sentence/paragraph	☐	☐
B.	The sound of the bombing in paragraphs 2 and 3	☐	☐
C.	The writer's feelings as he looks across London in paragraph 4	☐	☐
D.	The description of fires in paragraphs 5–7	☐	☐
E.	The sound of the planes in paragraph 8	☐	☐
F.	The sound of anti-aircraft guns in paragraph 9	☐	☐
G.	The description of incendiary bombs in paragraph 10	☐	☐
H.	The writer sums up the scene in paragraph 11	☐	☐
I.	The writer sums up his feelings in paragraphs 11 and 12	☐	☐

(2) Look again at your answers to question **(1)** above. Tick ✓ the four sections of the text which you have given the highest score.

  a Add the letters of your chosen elements (e.g. A, B) to the table below. ✎

  b For each section you have chosen, select a quotation from that part of the text which best shows how the writer's choices of ideas, language and structure engaged and interested you. ✎

Letter	Quotation

2 How do I select quotations?

To help you select the most effective quotations, you need to ask yourself some key questions.

Look again at the exam-style question:

Exam-style question

Analyse how the writer uses language and structure to <u>interest and engage</u> readers.

① Now look at a quotation from the text which you could use in your analysis. Answer the questions (A–D) around it.

A. Can I answer most or all of questions B, C and D?

If not, choose a different quotation which will help you answer the question.

B. Which words in the quotation has the writer used to create some kind of impact?

Do these words work together to create an impact? Or do they create different effects?

'London stabbed with great fires, shaken by explosions, its dark regions along the Thames sparkling with the pin points of white-hot bombs'

C. What do you notice about the sentence structure(s) in the quotation?

Is the sentence a long list, a short dramatic statement, or something else? What effect does it have?

D. What impact does the writer want these choices to have on the reader?

How do these choices help to engage the reader?

② Choose another quotation from the extract on page 10: one which will allow you to comment on the writer's choices and their impact on the reader. Annotate your chosen quotation with your comments on paper, using questions B to D to help you.

3 How do I develop my analysis?

When you focus on a quotation you have selected, you should aim to make your comments as detailed and specific as you can. Think about:

- commenting on the writer's choice of vocabulary
- commenting on the writer's choice of sentence structure
- being precise about the impact of the writer's choices on the reader.

1 Look closely at this quotation from the extract on page 10.

> It was a night when London was ringed and stabbed with fire.

Now look at three different students' comments on the ways in which the writer uses language to describe London in the quotation above. Annotate ✏ each comment, identifying what is effective about the analysis and what could be added or improved.

Student A:

☐

> It's really dramatic because it describes what happened in London and it sounds really bad. This makes the text more interesting and engaging for readers because it really describes it well and you can picture the scene.

Student B:

☐

> The word 'stabbed' makes it sound really dramatic.

Student C:

☐

> The writer uses a short sentence and the aggressive verb 'stabbed' to make it sound dramatic and violent.

2 Tick ✓ the student's comment above which you think makes the most effective analysis of the quotation. What has the writer of your chosen comment done well? Note down ✏ three things that you think make it the most successful analysis.

a ....

b ....

c ....

3 Look at this quotation from lines 5–7 of the extract.

Using your answers to question 2 to help you, write ✏ a sentence or two analysing how the writer's choices in the quotation make the text engaging and interesting.

> You could hear the boom, crump, crump, crump, of heavy bombs at their work of tearing buildings apart. They were not too far away.

....

....

....

....

Analysing a text

To write an effective analysis you need to do the following.

- Focus closely on the key words in the question: what are you being asked to analyse?
- Identify relevant parts of the text which will help you answer the question.
- Select quotations from those parts, making sure you can comment on them in detail.
- Develop your analysis of each quotation as fully and precisely as possible.

Look at the exam-style question.

Exam-style question

Analyse how the writer uses language and structure to interest and engage readers.

Support your views with detailed reference to the text.

(15 marks)

① Look at this paragraph from one student's response to the exam-style question above. Link 🖉 the annotations to the paragraph to show where the student has used each element of a successful paragraph of analysis.

quotation from the text

comments on vocabulary and/ or sentence structure choices

The writer's reaction to the attack is very surprising and even shocking for readers. He writes about 'the monstrous loveliness of that one single view of London'. The vocabulary in this sentence is one of the most engaging and interesting parts of the text. The adjective 'monstrous' presents the bombers as monsters and the people of London as their helpless victims but 'loveliness' suggests that the burning city is a beautiful sight. These mixed emotions of horror, excitement and beauty show what a strange and terrible experience it was.

comments precisely on the impact of these choices on readers

use key words from the question

② One way to structure a paragraph of analysis is to write it in three parts: point/evidence/explain. This writer has included all three elements, but not in that order. Is it effective? Write 🖉 a sentence or two explaining your ideas.

....

....

....

....

....

....

Your turn!

You are now going to write ✏️ your own answer to this exam-style question.

Exam-style question

Analyse how the writer uses language and structure to interest and engage readers.

Support your views with detailed reference to the text.

(15 marks)

---

(1) You should spend around 15–20 minutes on this type of question, so should aim to write three or four paragraphs.

a Use the planning space below to note ✏️ four quotations you could focus on in your answer. Remember to choose quotations which will give you opportunities to:

- analyse how the writer engages and interests readers
- analyse the impact of the writer's vocabulary and sentence structure choices
- explore the precise impact of those choices on readers.

1	
2	
3	
4	

b Annotate ✏️ the vocabulary and/or sentence structure choices in your quotations which you will write about in your answer. If you find it tricky to annotate any of your quotations, ask yourself:

- Have I chosen a good quotation?
- Are there better quotations which I could analyse more fully? If so, choose again.

(2) When you are happy with your choice of quotations and your annotation of them, write ✏️ your response to the exam-style question above on paper.

Review your skills

Check up

Review your response to the exam-style question on page 15. Tick ✓ the column to show how well you think you have done each of the following.

	Had a go ✓	Nearly there ✓	Got it! ✓
identified relevant parts of the text	☐	☐	☐
selected quotations	☐	☐	☐
analysed my chosen quotations	☐	☐	☐
focused my analysis on the keywords in the question	☐	☐	☐

Look over all of your work in this unit. Note down ✐ the three most important things to remember when you analyse a text.

1. ....

2. ....

3. ....

Need more practice?

Here is another exam-style question, this time relating to Text 1 on page 73: an extract from *The Final Problem*, a short story by Arthur Conan Doyle about the detective, Sherlock Holmes. You'll find some suggested points to refer to in the Answers section.

Exam-style question

In lines 1 to 8, how does the writer use language and structure to show the impact of the Reichenbach Falls on the narrator?

Support your views with reference to the text.

(6 marks)

How confident do you feel about each of these **skills?** Colour ✐ in the bars.

① How do I begin to analyse a text?   ☐☐☐☐

② How do I select quotations?   ☐☐☐☐

③ How do I develop my analysis?   ☐☐☐☐

Get started

Explain, comment on and analyse how writers use language and structure to achieve effects and influence readers (AO2)

③ Commenting on language

This unit will help you analyse a writer's use of language: the words that the writer has chosen to use in a text. The skills you will build are to:

- identify significant language choices in a text
- explore how the writer's language choices support the writer's intention
- analyse the impact of the writer's language choices.

In the exam you will face questions like the one below. This is about the text on page 18. This unit will prepare you to write your own response to this question, focusing on the writer's use of language (Unit 4 focuses on how to analyse the writer's use of structure).

Exam-style question

Analyse how the writer uses language and structure to engage and interest readers.

Support your views with detailed reference to the text.

(15 marks)

The three key questions in the **skills boosts** will help you comment on language.

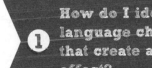
1 How do I identify language choices that create a specific effect?

2 How do I know what effect the writer is trying to create?

3 How do I analyse the writer's use of language?

Read the extract on page 18 from *Cider with Rosie*, the first volume of Laurie Lee's autobiography, written in 1959. You will tackle a 20th century non-fiction extract in the Reading section of your Paper 2 exam.

As you read, remember the following:

The impression which the writer is trying to create of the narrator and his surroundings in the extract.

Any language choices in the extract which you find surprising or effective.

In 1918, Laurie Lee and his family moved from a large town to a small village in the Gloucestershire countryside.

Text 1 Cider with Rosie, Laurie Lee

I was set down from the carrier's cart at the age of three; and there with a sense of bewilderment and terror my life in the village began.

The June grass, amongst which I stood, was taller than I was, and I wept. I had never been so close to grass before. It towered above me and all around me, each blade tattooed with tiger-skins of sunlight. It was knife-edged, dark, and a wicked green, thick as a forest and alive with grasshoppers that chirped and chattered and leapt through the air like monkeys.

I was lost and didn't know where to move. A tropic heat oozed up from the ground, rank with sharp odours of roots and nettles. Snow-clouds of elder-blossom banked in the sky, showering upon me the fumes and flakes of their sweet and giddy suffocation. High overhead ran frenzied larks, screaming, as though the sky were tearing apart.

For the first time in my life I was out of the sight of humans. For the first time in my life I was alone in a world whose behaviour I could neither predict nor fathom: a world of birds that squealed, of plants that stank, of insects that sprang about without warning. I was lost and I did not expect to be found again. I put back my head and howled, and the sun hit me smartly on the face, like a bully.

From this daylight nightmare I was awakened, as from many another, by the appearance of my sisters. They came scrambling and calling up the steep rough bank, and parting the long grass found me. Faces of rose, familiar, living; huge shining faces hung up like shields between me and the sky; faces with grins and white teeth (some broken) to be conjured up like genii with a howl, brushing off terror with their broad scoldings and affection. They leaned over me – one, two, three – their mouths smeared with red currants and their hands dripping with juice.

'There, there, it's all right, don't you wail any more. Come down 'ome and we'll stuff you with currants.'

And Marjorie, the eldest, lifted me into her long brown hair, and ran me jogging down the path and through the steep rose-filled garden, and set me down on the cottage doorstep, which was our home, though I couldn't believe it.

That was the day we came to the village, in the summer of the last year of the First World War. To a cottage that stood in a half-acre of garden on a steep bank above a lake; a cottage with three floors and a cellar and a treasure in the walls, with a pump and apple trees, syringa and strawberries, rooks in the chimneys, frogs in the cellar, mushrooms on the ceiling, and all for three and sixpence a week.

I don't know where I lived before then. My life began on the carrier's cart which brought me up the long slow hills to the village, and dumped me in the high grass, and lost me. I had ridden wrapped up in a Union Jack to protect me from the sun, and when I rolled out of it, and stood piping loud among the buzzing jungle of that summer bank, then, I feel, was I born. And to all the rest of us, the whole family of eight, it was the beginning of a life.

1 How do I identify language choices that create a specific effect?

You may be asked to identify examples of language that the writer has chosen to:

- create a particular mood
- show how someone in the text is feeling
- help the writer to make a point or explain an idea.

(1) Re-read the first two paragraphs of the extract on page 18. How would you sum up the narrator's feelings in these paragraphs in just one or two words? ✎

....

(2) Now look at these quotations from the first three paragraphs. Which **two** most clearly show how the narrator is feeling? Tick ✓ your choices.

1.	I was set down from the carrier's cart at the age of three;	☐
2.	there with a sense of bewilderment and terror my life in the village began.	☐
3.	The June grass, amongst which I stood, was taller than I was, and I wept.	☐
4.	I had never been so close to grass before.	☐
5.	It towered above me and all around me, each blade tattooed with tiger-skins of sunlight.	☐
6.	It was knife-edged, dark, and a wicked green, thick as a forest	☐
7.	alive with grasshoppers that chirped and chattered and leapt through the air like monkeys.	☐

(3) Look again at your answers to question (2).

- (a) In the quotations you ticked, circle (A) any words or phrases which show or suggest the narrator's feelings.
- (b) Annotate ✎ your chosen words or phrases from part (a) to explain why you chose them.

(4) Now answer this exam-style question ✎. You could use your answers to question (3) to help you.

Exam-style question

From lines 3–10, give **two** ways the narrator's language shows that he is feeling frightened.

(2 marks)

(a) ....

....

(b) ....

....

Unit 3 Commenting on language   19

② How do I know what effect the writer is trying to create?

When you think about an effect that the writer is using language to create, you first need to ask yourself:
- What is the writer's intention in this text?
- How are they trying to make me think or feel or react to their ideas?

① Look closely at this paragraph from the extract.

> For the first time in my life I was out of the sight of humans. For the first time in my life I was alone in a world whose behaviour I could neither predict nor fathom: a world of birds that squealed, of plants that stank, of insects that sprang about without warning. I was lost and I did not expect to be found again. I put back my head and howled, and the sun hit me smartly on the face, like a bully.

How does the **narrator** feel in this paragraph? Tick ✓ two words from the suggestions below.

frightened		intimidated		abandoned		confused	

threatened		upset		angry		sad		miserable	

② **a** What do you think the writer wants the **reader** to think and feel as they read this paragraph? Tick ✓ one word from the suggestions below.

humour		fear		tension		curiosity		terror	

sympathy		anger		**antipathy**		disgust	

antipathy: the opposite of sympathy: to dislike or feel hostility

b Which parts of the paragraph are most likely to make the reader think or feel that way? Underline Ⓐ two or three words or phrases or sentences in the paragraph above which help the writer to achieve that response.

c Write 🖉 a sentence or two explaining your choices in question **b**.

....

....

....

....

....

....

③ Now look at the rest of the extract on page 18. Note down 🖉 one or two words in answer to each of these questions:

a How do the writer's feelings change as the extract develops? ....

b How does the writer want the reader to think and feel as the extract develops? ....

c Which of the writer's choices of words, phrases or language features help the writer to achieve that response? ....

20 **Unit 3 Commenting on language**

3 How do I analyse the writer's use of language?

You can analyse the writer's use of language more closely by thinking about the ideas and associations that the writer's language choices create in the reader's mind. These are called their **connotations**.
For example:

The writer describes 'plants that stank'.

Meaning	Connotations	Effect
they smelt	terrible, rotten smell	suggests an uninviting, unpleasant situation

1. Look at this sentence from the extract on page 18. Think about the connotations of the word 'howled'.

   > I put back my head and howled, and the sun hit me smartly on the face, like a bully.

   a. What creature do you expect to 'howl'? 🖉 ....

   b. What does this suggest about the way the narrator sounds and feels? 🖉

   ....

   ....

   ....

   c. What impact might the word 'howl' have on the reader? Write 🖉 a sentence or two explaining your ideas.

   ....

   ....

   ....

2. Look again at the same sentence from the extract below, and think about the connotations of the underlined word.

   a. What does the writer mean? What ideas, thoughts and feelings does it create in your mind? How does it make you think about the sun and the narrator? Add your ideas to the boxes below. 🖉

   > I put back my head and howled, and the sun hit me smartly on the face, like a bully.

Meaning	Connotations	Effect

   b. What impact might the word 'bully' have on the reader? Write 🖉 a sentence or two explaining your ideas.

   ....

   ....

   ....

Commenting on language

To write an effective analysis of the writer's use of language you need to:

- think about the writer's different intentions in the text: how does he want the reader to respond to the ideas and events described in the extract?
- consider how the writer's language choices help the writer to achieve those intentions.
- analyse in detail the connotations and impact of some of the writer's most significant language choices in the extract.

Look at this exam-style question.

Exam-style question

Analyse how the writer uses language and structure to engage and interest readers.

Support your views with detailed reference to the text.

(15 marks)

(1) Carefully re-read the exam-style question above. Circle Ⓐ the **key words in the question**: those words which **either** tell you what you are being asked to do **or** you should include in every paragraph of your answer **or** both.

(2) Now look at a paragraph from one student's response to the question.

uses key words from the question

identifies the writer's intention

supported with evidence from the text

> The writer engages the reader's interest by creating sympathy for the narrator. For example, he describes how upset and threatened the narrator feels when he thinks he has been abandoned and will never see his family again. He describes how the narrator is surrounded by grass: 'It was knife-edged, dark, and a wicked green'. The word 'knife-edged' makes it sound sharp and dangerous and threatening and the word 'wicked' makes it sound evil and like it is trying to harm him. This language makes us feel sorry for the narrator because he is so young and he thinks he is in serious danger.

comments on connotations of language choices

comments on how this helps to achieve the writer's intention

Can you identify all the different things the student has included in this paragraph?

Link 🖉 the annotations to the paragraph to show where the student has included them.

Your turn!

You are now going to plan and write ✏ your own answer, focusing on the writer's use of language (Unit 4 focuses on how to analyse the writer's use of structure).

Exam-style question

Analyse how the writer uses language and structure to engage and interest readers.

Support your views with detailed reference to the text.

(15 marks)

(1) Think about the ways in which the writer tries to engage and interest readers in the extract. Note down ✏ some ways he does this.

> The writer engages and interests the reader by describing...

> The writer engages and interests the reader by including details of...

> The writer engages and interests the reader by writing about...

(2) Now look closely at the parts of the text where the writer does each of these things. Note down ✏ some key language choices (words and phrases) that help the writer to achieve these things.

(3) Note down ✏ some ideas which will help you analyse the writer's language choices. How do the connotations of each word or phrase contribute to the writer's intentions?

> This suggests...

> This has connotations of...

> This creates the impression of...

> This encourages the reader to feel...

(4) Use your ideas and planning above to write ✏ your response to the exam-style question above on paper.

Review your skills

Check up

Review your response to the exam-style question on page 23. Tick ✓ the column to show how well you think you have done each of the following.

	Had a go ✓	Nearly there ✓	Got it! ✓
identified significant language choices in the text	☐	☐	☐
explored how the writer's language choices support the writer's intention	☐	☐	☐
analysed the impact of the writer's language choices	☐	☐	☐

Look over all of your work in this unit. Note down ✐ the three most important things to remember when analysing the writer's use of words, phrases and language features.

1. ....

2. ....

3. ....

Need more practice?

Here is another exam-style question, this time relating to the Text 1 on page 73 from *The Final Problem*, a short story by Arthur Conan Doyle about the detective, Sherlock Holmes. This is the kind of question you can expect to tackle in Paper 1. You'll find some suggested points to refer to in the Answers section.

Exam-style question

How does the writer use language and structure to show Watson's reaction to being tricked?

Support your views with reference to the text.

(6 marks)

How confident do you feel about each of these **skills?** Colour ✐ in the bars.

1 How do I identify language choices that create a specific effect?

2 How do I know what effect the writer is trying to create?

3 How do I analyse the writer's use of language?

Get started

Explain, comment on and analyse how writers use language and structure to achieve effects and influence readers (AO2)

④ Commenting on structure

This unit will help you to comment on structure. The skills you will build are to:

• identify and comment on features of whole text structure

• identify and comment on the writer's choices of sentence structure

• develop your analysis of sentence structure.

In the exam you will face questions like the one below. This is about the text on page 26. At the end of the unit you will write your own response to this question, focusing on the writer's use of structure (Unit 3 focused on how to analyse the writer's use of language).

Exam-style question

Analyse how the writer uses language and structure to interest and engage readers.

Support your views with detailed reference to the text.   (15 marks)

The three key questions in the **skills boosts** will help you comment on structure.

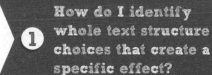
1 How do I identify whole text structure choices that create a specific effect?

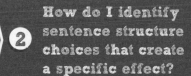
2 How do I identify sentence structure choices that create a specific effect?

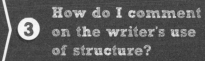
3 How do I comment on the writer's use of structure?

Read the extract on page 26 from a newspaper article. You will tackle a 21st century non-fiction extract in the Reading section of your Paper 2 exam.

As you read, remember the following: ✓

How has the writer selected ideas and information to engage and interest readers?

How has the writer structured the text and her sentences to add impact to the ideas and information?

This newspaper article appeared in the Mirror in 2015.

> **Text 1** Andrea Annear wrapped the world in a hug and made the human race a little kinder, Susie Boniface

It is always remarked upon when a celebrity does something for those less fortunate.

Perhaps it's because they're pretty, rich, and/or perfect; it seems so nice of them to notice people who aren't.

That's not to say the good works of celebrities aren't valuable. They have enormous reach and persuasive qualities, and can achieve a lot if they put their minds to it.

5 Now consider the case of Andrea Annear. She was born in about 1969 with Down's Syndrome, a condition which gave her slowed development, distinctive facial features, a weak heart and a lowered IQ.

She was in a children's home by the age of three, and there met another Down's sufferer, Paul Annear. His parents had given him up for fostering, and then his foster mother grew too old to cope, and so sent him to the home.

Down's had been known about for some time but the cause – an extra copy of a chromosome – was discovered 10 in 1959, just 10 years before Andrea was born. These two grew up in a world with little understanding of their problems.

Paul and Andrea grew up and fell in love as teenagers. But in 1996, when Andrea was about 26, she was moved out of the home to secure accommodation. She was at the higher end of the Down's spectrum, and was able to hold down a part-time job at a local hotel.

15 But the two were devastated at being apart, and had to persuade social workers to let them see each other.

She said later: 'I missed him. I heard music and I wanted to dance with him. If I felt sad inside my heart, there was no one to make me laugh any more. I wanted to see my friend, so I asked my carer if I could invite him over for tea.'

The pair fell into each other's arms the moment they met. Carer Eve Millar said: 'They had always been inseparable 20 at the children's home – and suddenly here they were, together again and loving every moment. Without each other, they existed. Together, they just shone.'

The pair were both committed Christians, and one day Paul went down on one knee and proposed. The couple told their carers they wanted to marry.

But they had to battle to persuade the authorities they had a right to do something the rest of us take for 25 granted. They were told they didn't have the mental capacity to understand the vows or the commitment.

At first they were fobbed off with a blessing held in their front room, but they continued to argue for a full church wedding, and saved up for rings, a dress and a suit.

Eventually, after much persuasion, they got their wish.

They honeymooned in Fuerteventura, and Paul got a job as a hotel porter. They lived together in a flat, with a carer 30 who popped in once a day to make sure they were okay. Last year they celebrated their 10th anniversary.

Andrea was not rich, or a Hollywood star or a great author. She had no fanbase to influence or millions to donate.

But what she and Paul did reaches all of us. They proved that being born different doesn't make you less human, and that disabilities are something to overcome and deal with rather than submit to.

They smashed the idea that 'people like them' were worthless. And they made it possible by quietly, persistently, 35 and thoroughly loving each other.

1 How do I identify whole text structure choices that create a specific effect?

To comment on a text's structure, you need to think about:

- the writer's **intention**
- how the ideas in the text are selected and ordered to achieve that intention
- other whole text features such as dialogue, quotes, tables, images etc.

> **intention:** the impact the writer wants the text to have on the reader

1. Why do you think the writer wrote the newspaper article on page 26? What impact does the writer want it to have on the reader? Sum up your ideas in **one** sentence. ✐

....

....

2. Which of the 18 paragraphs in the article help the writer to achieve the impact you identified in question ①? On the text on page 26, **tick** ✓ those that **do** and **cross** ✗ those that **do not**.

3. There are several ways in which a writer can decide to structure and present the ideas in a text.

   a. Tick ✓ any of the ways below which the writer uses in the text on page 26.

tell a story ☐	chronological order ☐	non-chronological order ☐

   | grouping related ideas ☐ | describes a problem, gives a solution ☐ | quotes ☐ |

   | a powerful conclusion brings the text's key ideas together ☐ | subheadings ☐ |

   | a thought-provoking introduction ☐ | numbered lists/bullet points ☐ |

   b. Annotate ✐ the text on page 26, identifying all the features you have ticked.

4. Most of the paragraphs in the article focus on Andrea Annear. Which ones do **not**? Why do you think the writer included these ideas in the article? ✐

....

....

....

5. Now think about the paragraphs which **do** focus on Andrea Annear. How has the writer structured them? Write ✐ a sentence explaining your ideas.

....

....

....

6. Now think about how some of the whole-text-structure choices you have identified on this page help the writer to **interest and engage readers**. Write ✐ a sentence or two explaining your ideas.

....

....

....

....

How do I identify sentence structure choices that create a specific effect?

To deliver information clearly, writers often choose to use sentences that are not too short and not too long, often beginning with a noun, noun phrase or pronoun followed by a verb. For example:

> She was in a children's home

> Paul and Andrea grew up

> They honeymooned in

Some sentences are structured to create impact and to help the writer achieve their intention.

1 To identify sentences that may have been crafted for effect rather than clarity, you could look out for sentences:

> A. that are much shorter than most

> C. that do not begin with a noun, noun phrase or pronoun

> B. that are much longer than most

> D. in which key information is not revealed until the end of the sentence.

Identify one of each of the above types of sentence in the text on page 26, annotating them A–D ✎.

2 Look carefully at these sentences from the article:

> Without each other, they existed. Together, they just shone.

The same meaning can be expressed in a completely different sentence structure with the addition of just one word:

> They existed without each other but they just shone together.

a Label at least three differences between the two versions above. Think about sentence length and word order. ✎

b Think about the ways in which the sentence length and structure of the original creates emphasis and impact which is lost in the other version. Write ✎ two or three sentences explaining how this emphasis and impact is created.

....

....

....

....

....

....

....

....

3 How do I comment on the writer's use of structure?

Writers often structure sentences to manipulate their impact and their emphasis.

1 a Look carefully at the six sentences from the article on page 26. Tick ✓ **three** sentences which you think have been structured to create a specific effect.

A. ☐ Now consider the case of Andrea Annear.

B. ☐ She was born in about 1969 with Down's Syndrome, a condition which gave her slowed development, distinctive facial features, a weak heart and a lowered IQ.

C. ☐ She was in a children's home by the age of three, and there met another Down's sufferer, Paul Annear.

D. ☐ His parents had given him up for fostering, and then his foster mother grew too old to cope, and so sent him to the home.

E. ☐ At first they were fobbed off with a blessing held in their front room, but they continued to argue for a full church wedding, and saved up for rings, a dress and a suit.

F. ☐ Eventually, after much persuasion, they got their wish.

b Using the suggestions below, write 🖉 about **one** of your chosen sentences, commenting on:
- the kind of **sentence structure** the writer has used • the **impact** of your chosen sentence
- how your chosen sentence helps the writer to achieve their **intention**.

Sentence structure	Impact	Intention
A short sentence	which adds emphasis,	emphasising that ordinary people can inspire us.
A longer sentence listing events or information	which highlights a key point or idea,	highlighting what Andrea had to overcome.
A sentence which begins with a key word or phrase	which provides descriptive detail,	highlighting what Andrea achieved in her life.
A sentence where key information is delayed to the end	which creates tension,	engaging the reader's interest in Andrea's story.

Sentence .... is ....

....

....

....

....

....

2 Identify one further sentence in the article on page 26. Annotate 🖉 your chosen sentence on paper, commenting on how it is structured, the impact of its structure and how it helps the writer to achieve their intention.

Commenting on structure

To comment successfully on structure, you need to explore:

- the selection and structure of ideas in the whole text
- the use of whole text features in the extract
- the impact of the whole text's structure and features on the reader
- sentence length and structure chosen for emphasis and/or impact
- the impact of those sentence structures on the reader.

Look at this exam-style question.

Exam-style question

Analyse how the writer uses language and structure to interest and engage readers.

Support your views with detailed reference to the text.

(15 marks)

① Circle Ⓐ the **key words in the question** that **either** tell you what you are being asked to do **or** that you should include in every paragraph of your answer **or** both.

② Now look at two students' comments on this quotation from the text.

> And they made it possible by quietly, persistently, and thoroughly loving each other.

Student A

In this final sentence of the article, the writer sums up her ideas about the power of love and how ordinary disabled people are and how ordinary people can inspire us. The writer engages the reader in the story of Andrea Annear and in the conclusion she makes about it.

Student B

The sentence is structured to delay the key phrase 'loving each other' to the very end of the sentence and the whole article. This helps to emphasise the importance of love to Paul and Andrea and its importance in engaging the reader in the ideas explored in the article.

Which of the two students' comments is the most effective? Write ✏ a sentence or two explaining your choice. Use the bullet point list of key features at the top of the page to help you.

....

....

....

....

....

....

Your turn!

You are now going to write (✐) your own answer, focusing on the writer's use of structure (Unit 3 focuses on how to analyse the writer's use of language).

Exam-style question

Analyse how the writer uses language and structure to interest and engage readers.

Support your views with detailed reference to the text. (15 marks)

① Note down (✐) **three** structural features you could include in your answer. These could be: features of whole text structure which help the writer to engage or interest readers **and/or** sentences whose structure helps the writer to engage or interest readers.

1.	2.	3.

② For each of the features or sentences, note down (✐) some ideas you could include in your analysis of their structure and/or impact on the reader.

1.	2.	3.

③ For each of the features or sentences, note down (✐) how their impact helps the writer to engage and interest the reader.

1.	2.	3.

④ Use your ideas and planning from questions ①–③ to write (✐) your response to the exam-style question above on paper.

Review your skills

Check up

Review your response to the exam-style question on page 31. Tick ⊘ the column to show how well you think you have done each of the following skills.

	Had a go ⊘	Nearly there ⊘	Got it! ⊘
identified whole text features	☐	☐	☐
commented on the impact of whole text features	☐	☐	☐
identified sentence structures crafted for effect	☐	☐	☐
commented on the impact of sentence structures	☐	☐	☐

Need more practice?

Here is another exam-style question, this time relating to another newspaper article, Text 3 on page 75 called *A Back Seat Education*. You'll find some suggested points to refer to in the Answers section ⊘.

Exam-style question

Analyse how the writer uses language and structure to interest and engage readers.

Support your views with detailed reference to the text.

(15 marks)

How confident do you feel about each of these **skills?** Colour ⊘ in the bars.

1 How do I identify whole text structure choices that create a specific effect?

2 How do I identify sentence structure choices that create a specific effect?

3 How do I comment on the writer's use of structure?

Explain, comment on and analyse how writers use language and structure to achieve effects and influence readers (AO2)

(5) Commenting on language and structure

This unit will help you comment on both language and structure together. The skills you will build are to:

- identify quotations in which the writer has made significant language and/or structure choices
- understand how language and structure work together to create impact
- structure and develop your analysis of language and structure.

In the exam you will face questions like the one below. This is about the text on page 34. At the end of the unit you will write your own response to this question.

Exam-style question

Analyse how the writer uses language and structure to interest and engage readers.

Support your views with detailed reference to the text.

(15 marks)

The three key questions in the **skills boosts** will help you comment on language and structure.

1 How do I select the most relevant quotations?

2 How do language and structure work together?

3 How do I comment on language and structure?

Read the extract on page 34 from *How to Survive the Exam Season*, a newspaper article published in 2015. You will tackle a 21st century non-fiction extract in the Reading section of your Paper 2 exam.

As you read, remember the following:

Remember the focus of the exam question you are preparing to respond to.

Think about the ways in which the writer tries to interest and engage readers.

Underline Ⓐ or tick ✓ any parts of the text which **you** find interesting.

This newspaper article appeared in the Guardian in May 2015.

Text 1 How to survive the exam season, Nell Frizzell

All over the country this month, GCSE pupils will be sitting down, once again, to slog through their exams. Whether it's the chorus of sniffing, the three hours of cramping fingers, the coldly sweating armpits or the hotly anticipated questions that never appear, exams are an **archetypal stress dream** for a reason. But I'm afraid they matter. They matter enormously.

5   But exams can also be a brilliant, concise, exciting time to show off your knowledge and make the most of your revision. It's a hoop, sure, but you might as well jump through it with grace. So, as GCSE season hits, here's my guide to surviving, even enjoying, exams.

1. This is not a trick

The first thing to remember with exams, is that they are a test, not a trick. This is your opportunity to show what
10   you know, not to be punished for what you don't.

Walking into an exam with that sort of positive attitude will not only help you make the most of the opportunity, it will also make you much less likely to feel nauseous before the papers have even been handed out.

2. If it works, then work it

I knew a boy who came to his AS-level maths exam wearing a white lab coat, simply because it made him feel
15   cleverer. A boy in a friend's science GCSE exam wore a pair of earplugs to muffle the maddening soundtrack of ticking clocks, sniffing classmates, squeaking chairs and sobbing companions. As a child I went into my English Sats exam clutching a small toy chicken in my sweaty little hand, after my mother told me it was a good luck token.

Exams are not the time for peer pressure. It is perfectly acceptable to admit that you've done some revision [and]
20   it is fine to wear your lucky underwear.

3. Adrenaline is your friend

As it happens, I was good at exams. Even without my lucky chicken. Because, basically, I love adrenaline. The rush of adrenaline as you're told to turn over your papers, the tingling in your feet as you walk up a row of empty wooden desks, the thump of your heart as the stopclock starts and the cold wash of nerves that floods your
25   stomach as you read through that first question are all your body's way of preparing to perform. And an exam is a performance.

Don't be scared of adrenaline, don't dread the rush of nerves; both are essential if you're going to write for an hour or remember the third row of the periodic table.

4. Everybody fails sometimes

30   Einstein had to re-sit his university entrance exam. I'm not saying that flunking exams is a failsafe route to fame, success and an understanding of intermolecular forces; but it doesn't necessarily mean the end of your career.

Retakes exist for a reason and, as anyone learning to kiss can tell you, you'll learn a lot from a failed attempt. Of course you should stay in, get plenty of sleep, eat a healthy breakfast and leave yourself plenty of time to get to the exam. But if things don't all go to plan, if you do spend the exam staring blank-brained at an empty page, then
35   at least your ability to recover will stand you in good stead for years, if not decades to come.

Good luck!

archetypal stress dream: typical of the kind of dream you have when feeling anxious or stressed

How do I select the most relevant quotations?

When you are asked to analyse the writer's use of language and structure, you need to look for examples of vocabulary, sentence structure and whole text structure that have been chosen to have a significant impact on the reader. Think about:

- how the whole text is structured
- short dramatic sentences emphasising ideas
- long sentences listing details or building a picture in the reader's mind
- sentences structured to give emphasis to key ideas
- powerful, emotive or evocative vocabulary choices.

(1) Not every quotation you select has to be about both language **and** structure. You could select quotes that are about one or the other.

Look at these four quotes from lines 1–6 of the article:

A. All over the country this month, GCSE pupils will be sitting down, once again, to slog through their exams.

B. Whether it's the chorus of sniffing, the three hours of cramping fingers, the coldly sweating armpits or the hotly anticipated questions that never appear, exams are an archetypal stress dream for a reason.

C. But I'm afraid they matter. They matter enormously.

D. But exams can also be a brilliant, concise, exciting time to show off your knowledge and make the most of your revision.

(a) Label 🖉 each quotation with a letter to show whether you could use them to comment on the writer's:

- language choice (L)   • sentence structure choice (S)   • both (B)   • neither (N).

(b) Look again at each of the quotations you labelled 'L', 'S' or 'B'. Underline Ⓐ the relevant parts of each quotation and annotate 🖉 them with your ideas about the impact of the writer's use of language and structure.

(2) Look again at the article on page 34. Underline Ⓐ **one** further quotation from **line 6 to the end of the article** which will allow you to comment on the writer's choice of language or structure or both.

Unit 5 Commenting on language and structure   35

② How do language and structure work together?

In the most effective texts, writers make sentence structure and language choices work together to help them achieve their **intention**.

> **intention:** the impact the writer wants the text to have on the reader

① Which of these would you identify as the **main** intention(s) of the writer of the article on page 34? **Rank** them in order, and/or add your own ideas. ✍

☐ | to entertain the reader | ☐ | to reassure anxious GCSE students | ☐ | to help students face the reality of GCSEs | ☐ | _____

② Now look at this quotation from line 4:

> But I'm afraid they matter. They matter enormously.

a Look again at your response to question ① above. Which of the writer's intentions do the sentences in the above quotation help to achieve? ✍

....

b The sentences in the quotation above have been carefully crafted. Which of the writer's choices in the quotation makes the strongest contribution to the writer's intention? Tick ✓ your answer.

A. Two short sentences emphasise the writer's point. ☐

B. Repetition of the key word 'matter' emphasises the writer's point. ☐

C. The adverb 'enormously' emphasises the writer's point. ☐

D. All of the above. ☐

③ Look at the **writer's** choice of vocabulary and sentence structure in the sentence below.

> The rush of adrenaline as you're told to turn over your papers, the tingling in your feet as you walk up a row of empty wooden desks, the thump of your heart as the stopclock starts and the cold wash of nerves that floods your stomach as you read through that first question are all your body's way of preparing to perform.

a Underline Ⓐ all the words or phrases in the sentence that suggest how GCSE students can expect to feel in their exams.

b How does the structure of this sentence, listing these feelings in a long sentence, help the writer to make her point? Write ✍ a sentence or two explaining your ideas.

....

....

....

....

....

....

....

③ How do I comment on language and structure?

To effectively analyse a text, you need to link your comments on language and structure and focus them on the question you are answering.

Look again at the exam-style question you saw at the start of the unit.

Exam-style question

Analyse how the writer uses language and structure to interest and engage readers.

① Now look at the sentences below, written by a student in response to the exam-style question.

Tick ✓ any that might help you answer the question because they comment on the writer's use of language or structure or refer to key words in the exam-style question.

A. ☐ Exams are not the time for peer pressure.

B. ☐ the thump of your heart... the cold wash of nerves

C. ☐ Some of the strongest key points are delivered using very blunt, simple language.

D. ☐ The writer uses lots of emotive language choices to describe the fear and anxiety of exams.

E. ☐ The writer structures this point in a short sentence to add emphasis.

F. ☐ The sentence structure effectively highlights this as a key point which the reader should take to heart.

G. ☐ The writer suggests what you should and shouldn't do or think to help you cope with GCSEs.

H. ☐ By referring to 'peer pressure' the writer is suggesting that you should do whatever works for you, regardless of what other people think.

② Look at the sentences that you have ticked. Use **some** or **all** of them to craft an effective paragraph of analysis in response to the question above. Aim to adapt and improve the sentences, linking them using adverbials or conjunctions like the ones below. 🖉

| in this way | however | for example | such as | although | because |

....

....

....

....

....

....

....

....

Commenting on language and structure

To write an effective analysis of the writer's use of language and structure, you need to:

- identify relevant quotations featuring significant language and/or structure choices
- explore the impact of the writer's choices
- structure your analysis carefully, linking your ideas and focusing on the question.

Look at this exam-style question.

Exam-style question

Analyse how the writer uses language and structure to interest and engage readers.

Support your views with detailed reference to the text.

(15 marks)

Look at a paragraph written by one student in response to the exam-style question above.

effective choice of quotation ☐

identifies the writer's intention ☐

analyses the impact of the writer's use of language ☐

> The writer uses quite a lot of humour in the article. For example, she describes some of the strange ways that students have coped with GCSEs. She describes one boy who wore earplugs to 'muffle the maddening soundtrack of ticking clocks, sniffing classmates, squeaking chairs and sobbing companions.' Positioning the phrase 'sobbing companions' at the end of this long sentence adds to the humour because it's the most extreme example of what you might hear in an exam.

analyses the impact of the writer's use of structure ☐

focuses the analysis on the question ☐

① Tick ✓ all those key features which you can identify in the response and link ✐ them to the paragraph. Cross ✗ any that are missing from the paragraph.

② Use your ideas to develop and improve the paragraph ✐. You could either adjust the paragraph above or re-draft it on paper.

Your turn!

You are now going to write your own answer in response to the exam-style question.

Analyse how the writer uses language and structure to interest and engage readers.

Support your views with detailed reference to the text.

(15 marks)

You should spend around 20–25 minutes on this question so should aim to write three or four paragraphs.

(1) Use the space below to note down 🖉 the three quotations from the text on page 34 which you feel you can analyse most thoroughly and effectively.

1.

2.

3.

(2) Annotate 🖉 your chosen quotations, identifying and noting:
- key language and/or structure choices
- the intended impact of those choices on readers
- how those choices help the writer to achieve her intention and so engage and interest readers.

(3) Now write 🖉 your response to the exam-style question above on paper.

Review your skills

Check up

Review your response to the exam-style question on page 39. Tick ✓ the column to show how well you think you have done each of the following.

	Not quite ✓	Nearly there ✓	Got it! ✓
identified relevant quotations	☐	☐	☐
identified significant language and structure choices	☐	☐	☐
commented on the impact of language and structure choices	☐	☐	☐

Look over all of your work in this unit. Note down ✏ the three things you find most challenging about analysing a writer's use of language and structure. Rank them from 1 (the most challenging) to 3 (the least challenging).

1. .... ☐

2. .... ☐

3. .... ☐

Need more practice?

Here is another exam-style question, this time relating to Text 2 on page 74: an extract from *I Know Why The Caged Bird Sings* by Maya Angelou. You'll find some suggested points to refer to in the Answers section ✏.

Exam-style question

Analyse how the writer uses language and structure to interest and engage readers.

Support your views with detailed reference to the text.

(15 marks)

How confident do you feel about each of these **skills?** Colour ✏ in the bars.

1 How do I select the most relevant quotations?

2 How do language and structure work together?

3 How do I comment on language and structure?

⑥ Evaluating a text

This unit will help you evaluate texts. The skills you will build are to:

- identify the writer's intentions
- identify where in the text the writer has attempted to achieve that intention
- develop your analysis of the writer's choices and their impact on the reader
- develop your evaluation of how successfully the writer has achieved their intention and its impact on the reader.

In the exam you will face questions like the one below. This is about the text on page 42. This unit will prepare you to write your own response to this question.

Exam-style question

In this extract, there is an attempt to create a sense of danger.

Evaluate how successfully this is achieved.

Support your views with detailed reference to the text.

(15 marks)

The three key questions in the **skills boosts** will help you prepare your response.

① **How do I identify where the writer has tried to achieve their intention?**

② **How do I analyse the writer's intention?**

③ **How do I evaluate the writer's success in achieving their intention?**

Read the extract on page 42 from *The Phantom Coach*, a ghost story written in 1864 by Amelia Edwards. You will tackle a 19th century fiction extract in the Reading section of your Paper 1 exam.

As you read, remember the following: ✓

If you lose understanding of the extract, stop and re-read from the last sentence or paragraph that you clearly understood.

Mark or underline Ⓐ any parts of the extract relevant to the question you are going to answer. So, here, mark where you feel the writer is attempting to create a sense of danger.

Think about how the story might develop after the end of the extract: are there suggestions in the extract that the narrator may encounter danger later in the story? Mark the extract to indicate these.

In the opening of this ghost story, the narrator remembers a time when he was alone and lost.

Text 1 The Phantom Coach, Amelia Edwards

It was just twenty years ago, and within a day or two of the end of the **grouse season**. I had been out all day with my gun, and had had no sport to speak of. The wind was due east; the month, December; the place, a bleak wide moor in the far north of England. And I had lost my way. It was not a pleasant place in which to lose one's way, with the first feathery flakes of a coming snowstorm just fluttering down upon the heather, and the **leaden** evening
5 closing in all around. I shaded my eyes with my hand, and stared anxiously into the gathering darkness, where the purple moorland melted into a range of low hills, some ten or twelve miles distant. Not the faintest smoke-wreath, not the tiniest cultivated patch, or fence, or sheep-track, met my eyes in any direction. There was nothing for it but to walk on, and take my chance of finding what shelter I could, by the way. So I shouldered my gun again, and pushed wearily forward; for I had been on foot since an hour after daybreak, and had eaten nothing since
10 breakfast.

Meanwhile, the snow began to come down with ominous steadiness, and the wind fell. After this, the cold became more intense, and the night came rapidly up. As for me, my prospects darkened with the darkening sky, and my heart grew heavy as I thought how my young wife was already watching for me through the window of our little inn parlour, and thought of all the suffering in store for her throughout this weary night. We had been married
15 four months, and, having spent our autumn in the Highlands, were now lodging in a remote little village situated just on the verge of the great English moorlands. We were very much in love, and, of course, very happy. This morning, when we parted, she had implored me to return before dusk, and I had promised her that I would. What would I not have given to have kept my word!

Even now, weary as I was, I felt that with a supper, an hour's rest, and a guide, I might still get back to her before
20 midnight, if only guide and shelter could be found.

And all this time, the snow fell and the night thickened. I stopped and shouted every now and then, but my shouts seemed only to make the silence deeper. Then a vague sense of uneasiness came upon me, and I began to remember stories of travellers who had walked on and on in the falling snow until, wearied out, they were **fain** to lie down and sleep their lives away. Would it be possible, I asked myself, to keep on thus through all the long
25 dark night? Would there not come a time when my limbs must fail, and my resolution give way? When I, too, must sleep the sleep of death. Death! I shuddered. How hard to die just now, when life lay all so bright before me! How hard for my darling, whose whole loving heart but that thought was not to be borne! To banish it, I shouted again, louder and longer, and then listened eagerly. Was my shout answered, or did I only fancy that I heard a far-off cry? I halloed again, and again the echo followed. Then a wavering speck of light came suddenly out of the dark, shifting,
30 disappearing, growing momentarily nearer and brighter. Running towards it at full speed, I found myself, to my great joy, face to face with an old man and a lantern.

grouse season: the time of year during which grouse may be hunted
leaden: made of lead, a heavy grey metal
fain: willing, happy

1 How do I identify where the writer has tried to achieve their intention?

In every written text, the writer has an **intention**. Some evaluation tasks clearly state the intention which you must evaluate. Other tasks ask you to evaluate how the writer attempts to engage and interest the reader. In order to answer both types of task successfully, you need to **identify the writer's intention** and **where in the text the writer has attempted to achieve it.**

> **intention:** the impact the writer wants the text to have on the reader

1. Think about the impact the writer might want the opening of this or any ghost story to have on the reader. Tick ✓ any that you can find evidence for in the text and note the evidence on the table. Add your own ideas on the blank rows. ✎

✓	Intention	Evidence
	create a sense of danger	
	build tension	
	create an unsettling atmosphere	
	engage the reader	

2. Look at some of the different elements the writer has included in the story.

   a. Tick ✓ any which you think contribute to the writer's intention to create a sense of danger:

Narrator has been hunting	Narrator's wife expects him home
Narrator is lost	Narrator shouts for help
Narrator is hungry and tired	Narrator thinks of others who have died in the snow
The weather	Narrator thinks he hears a sound
The time of day	Narrator sees a light
The setting	Narrator meets an old man

   b. Identify and annotate ✎ where in the text the writer has included the details you have ticked in part **a** above.

3. Write ✎ a sentence or two summing up:
   - how the sense of danger rises or falls in the extract – use your answers to **1** to help.
   - the elements the writer uses to create a sense of danger – use your answers to **2** to help.

....

....

....

....

....

....

2 How do I analyse the writer's intention?

Your evaluation should **analyse how** the writer's choices of language and structure contribute to their intention. It should **also** comment on the impact that these choices have on the reader.

1 Look closely at this quotation from the extract:

> Death! I shuddered. How hard to die just now, when life lay all so bright before me!

a What impact does the writer intend these sentences to have on the reader?
Circle Ⓐ any of the suggestions below and add your own idea in the empty box.

anxiety	excitement	impatience	sympathy	annoyance	admiration

b How do the writer's choices in the quotation above contribute to that impact? Note 🖉 your ideas below.

i. The exclamation: Death!

ii. The choice of verb shuddered .

iii. The contrast of Death! and life which lay all so bright before me!

2 Use the notes you made above to write 🖉 two or three sentences analysing how the writer's choices in this quotation create a sense of danger and the impact these choices have on the reader.

....

....

....

....

....

3 Underline Ⓐ another quotation in the extract which you feel contributes to the writer's intention of creating a sense of danger. Write 🖉 two or three sentences, analysing how its language and structure contributes to that intention and its impact on the reader.

....

....

....

....

....

③ How do I evaluate the writer's success in achieving their intention?

An effective evaluation should explore **how** the writer has achieved their intention, its impact on the reader **and how effectively** the writer has achieved this.

① In each of the quotations you choose and the comments you make in your evaluation, you need to think about how successfully the writer of the text achieves their intention.

a Choose ✓ **one** of the quotations below which you feel:
- contributes to the writer's intention of creating a sense of danger
- has a significant impact on the reader
- will allow you to comment on the writer's choices of language and/or sentence structure.

| my prospects darkened with the darkening sky, and my heart grew heavy | □ | all this time, the snow fell and the night thickened | □ | a wavering speck of light came suddenly out of the dark, shifting, disappearing, growing momentarily nearer and brighter | □ |

b Focusing on your chosen quotation, underline Ⓐ any of the writer's choices of language and/ or sentence structure which you think are significant.

② Use these key questions and phrases to help you write 🖉 about the quotation you chose above.

What does the writer do?		How successfully?	What impact does this have on the reader?	
	suggests...	effectively		feels...
The writer	implies...	successfully		experiences...
The author	creates...	clearly	The reader	believes...
The text	describes...	strongly		is encouraged to...
The extract	emphasises...	powerfully		is led to...
	conveys...	vividly		is manipulated...

For example:

> The writer powerfully conveys a sense of the narrator's isolation: 'Not the faintest smoke-wreath, not the tiniest cultivated patch, or fence, or sheep-track, met my eyes in any direction.' The writer has structured this sentence as a list to emphasise the emptiness and desolation of this landscape, creating a sense of danger and encouraging the reader to feel concern and sympathy.

Write 🖉 your own response to your chosen quotation here.

....

....

....

....

....

....

How do I evaluate text?

To successfully evaluate a text, you need to:

- identify the writer's intentions (one of which may be stated in the exam question you are answering)
- identify where in the text the writer has attempted to achieve their intention(s)
- select detailed references to the text which support your ideas and allow you to comment on the writer's choices
- explore the writer's choices closely, focusing on **how** the writer has achieved their intention, its impact on the reader, and **how successfully** the writer has achieved this.

Now look at this exam-style question.

Exam-style question

In this extract, there is an attempt to create a sense of danger.

Evaluate how successfully this is achieved.

Support your views with detailed reference to the text.

(15 marks)

Then look at a paragraph from one student's response to it.

focuses on a specific element of the text: the setting

uses key words from the question

evidence from the text

comments on vocabulary and/ or sentence structure choices

At the beginning of the extract, the writer sets the scene. She immediately creates a strong sense of danger by describing 'a bleak wide moor'. The adjectives 'bleak' and 'wide' powerfully suggest the narrator is in the middle of nowhere. The writer then follows this long, descriptive sentence with the short sentence 'And I had lost my way.' to dramatically emphasise the danger he is in. This effectively encourages the reader to expect the narrator's situation to become even more dangerous.

comments on how this helps to achieve the writer's intention

comments on the impact of the text on the reader

uses evaluative language to comment on the writer's success in achieving her intention

Can you identify all the different things the student has included in this paragraph? Link 🖉 the annotations in the boxes to the paragraph to show where the student has included them.

Your turn!

You are now going to write your own answer in response to the exam-style question.

Exam-style question

In this extract, there is an attempt to create a sense of danger.

Evaluate how successfully this is achieved.

Support your views with detailed reference to the text.

(15 marks)

Before you write your response, complete the tasks below to help you prepare.

(1) You should spend around 25 minutes on this question, so should aim to write four or five paragraphs. Note down 🖉 below the different elements of the extract which you will focus on in each paragraph.

Paragraph 1.

Paragraph 2.

Paragraph 3.

Paragraph 4.

(2) Select the quotations you will explore in each paragraph. You could underline (A) them in the extract on page 42 and add the line number of each quotation to your notes above.

(3) Think about the comments you will make on the writer's choices in each paragraph. Annotate 🖉 the quotations you have selected on the extract, identifying key vocabulary and sentence structure choices which contribute to the writer's success in creating a sense of danger.

(4) Now write 🖉 your response to the exam-style question above on paper.

Review your skills

Check up

Review your response to the exam-style question on page 47. Tick ✓ the column to show how well you think you have done each of the following.

	Not quite ✓	Nearly there ✓	Got it! ✓
identified elements of the text which create a sense of danger	☐	☐	☐
identified relevant textual references	☐	☐	☐
commented in detail on the writer's choices	☐	☐	☐
commented in detail on the impact of the writer's choices on the reader	☐	☐	☐
evaluated the writer's success in achieving their intention	☐	☐	☐

Need more practice?

Here is another exam-style question, this time relating to the extract from *The Final Problem* on page 73. You'll find some suggested points to refer to in the Answers section ✐.

Exam-style question

In this extract there is an attempt to create drama and tension.

Evaluate how successfully this is achieved.

Support your views with detailed reference to the text.

(15 marks)

How confident do you feel about each of these **skills**? Colour ✐ in the bars.

1 How do I identify where the writer has tried to achieve their intention?

2 How do I analyse the writer's intention?

3 How do I evaluate the writer's success in achieving their intention?

(7) Synthesising and comparing

This unit will help you synthesise information and ideas from two texts and compare them. The skills you will build are to:

- identify **explicit** differences and similarities in two texts
- identify differences and similarities that are **implied** in two texts
- synthesise and compare the differences or similarities in two texts.

In the exam you will face questions like the one below. This is about the texts on page 50. At the end of the unit you will write your own response to this question.

Exam-style question

This question is about Text 1 and Text 2. Refer to both texts in your answers.

The two texts show the narrator's experiences with elderly people.

What similarities do the narrators share in these texts?

Use evidence from both texts to support your answer.

(6 marks)

The three key questions in the **skills boosts** will help you synthesise and compare similarities or differences in two texts.

1 How do I begin to identify similarities or differences?

2 How do I compare implied ideas?

3 How do I synthesise similarities or differences and compare them?

Read the extracts on page 50 from Clive James' autobiography *Unreliable Memoirs*, published in 1980, and from Sally Magnusson's account of her mother's dementia, *Where Memories Go*, published in 2014. You will tackle one 20th century non-fiction extract and one 21st century non-fiction extract in the Reading section of your Paper 2 exam.

As you read, remember the following:

Each of the narrator's experiences with elderly people.

Any similarities or differences between the narrators and their experiences with elderly people.

The writer remembers his grandfather, whom he lived with when he was very young.

Text 1 Unreliable Memoirs, Clive James

I remember him as a tall, barely articulate source of smells. The principal smells were of mouldy cloth, mothballs, seaweed, powerful tobacco and the tars that collect in the stem of a very old pipe. When he was smoking he was invisible. When he wasn't smoking he was merely hard to pick out in the gloom. You could track him down by listening for his constant, low-pitched, incoherent mumble. From his carpet slippers to his moustache was twice
5 as high as I could reach. The moustache was **saffron** with nicotine. Everywhere else he was either grey or tortoise-shell mottle. His teeth were both.

I remember he bared them at me one Christmas dinner. It was because he was choking on a coin in a mouthful of plum pudding. It was the usual Australian Christmas dinner, taking place in the middle of the day. Despite the temperature being 100 °F in the shade, there had been the full panoply of ragingly hot food, topped off
10 with a volcanic plum pudding smothered in scalding custard. My mother had naturally spiced the pudding with **sixpences and threepenny bits**, called zacs and trays respectively. Grandpa had collected one of these in the oesophagus. He gave a protracted, strangled gurgle which for a long time we all took to be the beginning of some anecdote. Then Aunt Dot bounded out of her chair and hit him in the back. By some miracle she did not snap his calcified spine. Coated with black crumbs and custard, the zac streaked out of his mouth like a **dum-dum** and
15 ricocheted off a tureen.

saffron: yellow
sixpences and threepenny bits: coins
dum-dum: a kind of bullet

The writer, Sally Magnusson, is visiting her mother in hospital. Her mother has Alzheimer's disease, a condition which mainly affects the elderly, causing a loss of mental ability. In this extract, Sally and her mother overhear a physiotherapist assessing another elderly patient.

Text 2 Where Memories Go, Sally Magnusson

The physio makes his way to the next bed at the bottom of the ward, where the loud Croatian lady has been replaced by Janet, who has a few brown teeth, a cut-glass accent and advanced dementia. Behind her curtain we hear him conducting a not-so-discreet mental test.

'Do you know what hospital you're in?' he asks.

5 No reply.

'All right. Do you know the name of the Prime Minister?'

You are listening avidly.

'Arthur?' the poor woman ventures.

'Not Arthur' says the physio, raising his voice. 'DO YOU KNOW WHO THE PRIME MINISTER IS?'

10 The rest of us wait with bated breath. Not having a clue yourself, you hiss, 'Well you hurry up and tell us then if you're so clever.'

Even as I try to stifle the giggles, I know that Janet represents our future.

Later I catch you gazing intently at the bed opposite. 'What is that cat doing over there?' you remark after a while.

'What cat?'

15 'That cat. Nice ginger cat, like Margaret's. In fact, I think it is Margaret's.'

'No, Mum, it's that lady's catheter bag. To collect her urine. You've got one, too. Look.'

'But mine doesn't look the same as hers.'

'No, hers has got more in it.'

'But what about those ears? That cat has got ears.'

20 It was probably the delirium, but who cares? It was the best laugh we had had in days.

1 How do I begin to identify similarities or differences?

Identifying **explicit** ideas and information in the two texts is the first stage in beginning to compare them.

> **explicit:**
> clearly stated

① Look at one student's notes, summarising all of the information and detail explicitly stated in the two texts on page 50.

Text 1: Unreliable Memoirs

a. The narrator is writing about when he was a child.

b. The text is about the narrator's elderly grandfather.

c. His grandfather makes a lot of smells.

d. His grandfather smokes heavily.

e. His grandfather mumbles and is difficult to understand.

f. His grandfather has discoloured teeth.

g. His grandfather choked on a coin one Christmas.

Text 2: Where Memories Go

a. The narrator is writing about when she was an adult.

b. The text is about the narrator's elderly mother and another elderly woman in hospital called Janet.

c. Janet has advanced dementia.

d. The doctor tests Janet's mental skills.

e. Janet is confused. She does not know where she is or the name of the prime minister.

f. The narrator's mother does not know the name of the prime minister.

g. The narrator's mother thinks another patient's catheter bag is a ginger cat.

h. The narrator and her mother laugh at her mistake.

Draw ✏ a line linking any detail from Text 1 ✏ to any detail from Text 2 which shows a similarity between the two texts. Label these lines 'S'. Now draw lines in a different colour linking any detail from text 1 that is different to text 2. Labels these linking lines 'D'.

② Write ✏ a sentence or two, summarising the similarities and differences in the two extracts.

....

....

....

2 How do I compare implied ideas?

Once you have identified any **explicit** similarities or differences in the texts, you need to focus on what you can **infer** from the texts which will help you to answer the question.

① Look closely at the quotations below, taken from the texts on page 50.

Tick ✓ any of the quotations from which you can infer information or ideas about the narrator. Annotate 🖉 them with your ideas.

Text 1: Unreliable Memoirs	Text 2: Where Memories Go
A. I remember him as a tall, barely articulate source of smells. ☐	F. 'All right. Do you know the name of the Prime Minister?' You are listening avidly. 'Arthur?' the poor woman ventures. ☐
B. You could track him down by listening for his constant, low-pitched, incoherent mumble. ☐	G. 'Not Arthur' says the physio, raising his voice. 'DO YOU KNOW WHO THE PRIME MINISTER IS?' ☐
C. He gave a protracted, strangled gurgle which for a long time we all took to be the beginning of some anecdote. ☐	H. Not having a clue yourself, you hiss, 'Well you hurry up and tell us then if you're so clever.' ☐
D. By some miracle she did not snap his calcified spine. ☐	I. Even as I try to stifle the giggles, I know that Janet represents our future. ☐
E. Coated with black crumbs and custard, the zac streaked out of his mouth like a **dum-dum** and ricocheted off a tureen. ☐	J. 'But what about those ears? That cat has got ears.' ☐
	K. It was probably the delirium, but who cares? It was the best laugh we had had in days. ☐

② In what ways are the narrators of the two texts similar or different?

a Circle Ⓐ **one** of the boxed words in each of the sentences below to sum up the similarities or differences in the family relationships described in the two texts.

				Text 1 quote	Text 2 quote
Both	Neither	One	of the narrators show(s) respect for the elderly.		
Both	Neither	One	of the narrators use(s) humour.		
Both	Neither	One	of the narrators laugh(s) **at** the elderly.		
Both	Neither	One	of the narrators laugh(s) **with** the elderly.		

b Choose a quote from **each** of the texts above as evidence to support your answers. Write 🖉 the letter of your chosen quotations at the end of each sentence.

3 How do I synthesise similarities or differences and compare them?

To effectively synthesise and compare information and ideas from two texts, you must make sure you are selecting information which is relevant to the question you are answering.

(1) Look again at the exam-style question you saw at the start of this unit.

Exam-style question

The two texts show the narrator's experiences with elderly people.

What similarities do the narrators share in these texts?

Which of these points are relevant to the question above? Tick ✓ them.

A. The narrator of Text 1 tells a humorous story about an elderly relative suggesting that he thinks the problems of old age can be funny. ☐

B. The narrator of Text 2 tells a humorous story about an elderly relative suggesting that she is able to laugh at the difficulties her mother is experiencing. ☐

C. The narrator of Text 1 describes his grandfather's physical appearance in some detail. ☐

D. The narrator of Text 2 does not describe her mother's physical appearance at all. ☐

E. The narrator of Text 1 focuses on the problems that his grandfather's old age caused, mainly for the rest of the family which shows he is not very sympathetic to his grandfather. ☐

F. The narrator of Text 2 focuses on the problems that her mother is experiencing and writes about 'our future' which suggests she sees them as problems that they will share. ☐

(2) Look again at the points you ticked above. Use them to write ✎ sentences about the similarities shared by the narrators of the two texts.

You can **link** comments on the similarities and differences in texts using words and phrases such as

| Similarly... | In the same way... | However... | On the other hand... | ...whereas... | ...but... |

or **synthesise** the similarities in two texts using words such as | Both... | Neither... | Each... |

....

....

....

....

....

....

....

Unit 7 Synthesising and comparing 53

Synthesising and comparing

To compare two texts, synthesising key information effectively, you need to:

- identify relevant information and ideas which are explicitly stated in the texts
- identify relevant information and ideas which are implied in the texts
- synthesise the relevant information and ideas from the texts to make relevant and valid comparisons.

Look at this exam-style question.

Exam-style question

This question is about Text 1 and Text 2. Refer to both texts in your answers.

The two texts show the narrator's experiences with elderly people.

What similarities do the narrators share in these texts?

Use evidence from both texts to support your answer.

(6 marks)

(1) Now look at a paragraph from one student's response to the exam-style question above.

> Both of the narrators are very honest about their relatives and their problems. For example, in Text 2 the narrator describes her mother not knowing who the prime minister is and mistaking a catheter bag for a ginger cat. In Text 1, however, the narrator is so honest he is almost cruel about his grandpa which makes me think he is using the story to make the reader laugh.

(a) Here are the key features of an effective answer. **Cross** ⊗ the key features of an effective answer which this student **has not** achieved in this paragraph and **tick** ✓ the key features which this student **has** achieved.

A. Focuses comments closely on the question.

B. Links or synthesises the different comments on the two texts.

C. Uses a relevant quotation or textual reference as evidence from each text.

(b) Annotate ✐ the paragraph to show which parts of the paragraph achieve which key feature.

Your turn!

You are now going to write your own answer in response to the exam-style question.

This question is about Text 1 and Text 2. Refer to both texts in your answers.

The two texts show the narrator's experiences with elderly people.

What similarities do the narrators share in these texts?

Use evidence from both texts to support your answer. **(6 marks)**

(1) You should spend 10–15 minutes on this kind of question, so should aim to write 🖉 two or three paragraphs. Use the space below to plan three paragraphs.

	Similarities	Text 1: Evidence	Text 2: Evidence
1			
2			
3			

(2) Now write 🖉 your response to the exam-style question above on paper.

Review your skills

Check up

Review your response to the exam-style question on page 55. Tick ✓ the column to show how well you think you have done each of the following.

	Not quite ✓	Nearly there ✓	Got it! ✓
identified **explicit** differences and similarities in two texts	☐	☐	☐
identified differences and similarities that are **implied** in two texts	☐	☐	☐
synthesised and compared the differences or similarities in two texts	☐	☐	☐

Need more practice?

Here is another exam-style question, this time relating to Text 2 on page 74: an extract from Maya Angelou's autobiography, *I Know Why The Caged Bird Sings*, published in 1969, and Text 3 on page 75: *A Back Seat Education*, a newspaper article published in 2016. You'll find some suggested points to refer to in the Answers section.

Exam-style question

This question is about Text 1 and Text 2. Refer to both texts in your answers.

The two texts show young people in different situations.

What similarities do the young people share in these texts?

Use evidence from both texts to support your answer.

(6 marks)

How confident do you feel about each of these **skills?** Colour 🖉 in the bars.

1 How do I begin to identify similarities or differences?

2 How do I compare implied ideas?

3 How do I synthesise similarities or differences and compare them?

(8) Comparing ideas and perspectives

This unit will help you learn how to compare the writers' ideas and perspectives in two texts. The skills you will build are to:

- identify the writer's ideas and perspectives
- identify similarities and differences in the ideas and perspectives in two texts
- develop a comparison of the ways in which the writers convey their ideas and perspectives
- structure a comparison of the writer's ideas and perspectives in two texts.

In the exam you will face questions like the one below. This is about the texts on page 58. At the end of the unit you will write your own response to this question.

Exam-style question

Compare how the writers of Text 1 and Text 2 present their ideas and perspectives about the natural world.

Support your answer with detailed references to the texts.

(14 marks)

Before you tackle the question you will work through three key questions in the **skills boosts** to help you compare the writers' ideas and perspectives.

 1 How do I identify and compare relevant ideas and perspectives?

 2 How do I develop my comparison of ideas and perspectives?

 3 How do I structure my comparison?

Read the extracts on page 58 from *The Lost Continent* by Bill Bryson, published in 1989, and *The Outrun* by Amy Liptrot, published in 2016. You will tackle two non-fiction extracts, one from the 20th century and one from the 21st century, in the Reading section of your Paper 2 exam.

As you read, remember the following:

The writer's ideas and perspectives in the two texts: how do they describe and respond to these wonders of the natural world?

Any similarities or differences between the two writers' ideas and perspectives.

The writer describes a visit to the Grand Canyon in the USA.

Text 1 The Lost Continent, Bill Bryson

Nothing prepares you for the Grand Canyon. No matter how many times you read about it or see it pictured, it still takes your breath away. Your mind, unable to deal with anything on this scale, just shuts down and for many long moments you are a human vacuum, without speech or breath, but just a deep, inexpressible awe that anything on this earth could be so vast, so beautiful, so silent. Even children are stilled by it. I was a particularly talkative
5   and obnoxious child, but it stopped me cold. I can remember rounding a corner and standing there agog while a mouthful of half-formed jabber just rolled backwards down my throat, forever unuttered.

The scale of the Grand Canyon is almost beyond comprehension. It is ten miles across, a mile deep, 180 miles long. You could set the Empire State Building down in it and still be thousands of feet above it. Indeed you could set the whole of Manhattan down inside it and you would still be so high above it that buses would be like ants
10   and people would be invisible, and not a sound would reach you. The thing that gets you – that gets everyone – is the silence. The Grand Canyon just swallows sound. The sense of space and emptiness is overwhelming. Nothing happens out there. Down below you on the canyon floor, far, far away, is the thing that carved it: the Colorado River. It is 300 feet wide, but from the canyon's lip it looks thin and insignificant. It looks like an old shoelace. Everything is dwarfed by this mighty hole.

Aged 30, Amy Liptrot gave up drinking alcohol, left her boyfriend and moved from London back to her childhood home on the Orkney Islands, a remote group of islands off the north coast of Scotland. In this extract, she describes watching the Northern Lights, or Aurora Borealis, known in Orkney as the Merry Dancers: a natural light display in the night sky, rarely seen in Britain.

Text 2 The Outrun, Amy Liptrot

Just outside the front door of Rose Cottage, with the house lights turned out, is a perfect spot to watch the aurora: an unobscured northern **vista**. About 75 per cent of my view is sky, and when I tip my head back, 100 per cent. In my first couple of weeks on **Papay**, I see the Merry Dancers more clearly than I ever have before. I let my eyes adjust to the dark for the time it takes to smoke one cigarette then say, 'Bloody hell,' out loud. In the past I have
5   seen a greenish-tinged, gently glowing arc, low across the north, but tonight the whole sky is alive with shapes: white 'searchlights' beaming from behind the horizon, dancing waves directly above and slowly, thrillingly, blood red blooms. It's brighter than a full moon and the birds, curlews and geese, are noisier than they usually are at this time of night, awakened by a false dawn. There is static in the air and it's an unusual kind of light, the eerie glow of a floodlit stadium or a picnic eaten in car headlights.

10   I keep going out during the evening to see if the lights are still there, while following photos being posted online and talking with friends on the Orkney Mainland or in the south about what we are watching.

Often at night I have sat up in bed circling my ex's abandoned online profiles. On Google Streetview the branches are bare on the tree in front of the flat we used to share. I long for him to know I'm doing better but I won't be truly better until I no longer want him to know. But tonight I'm wild on Northern Lights. I'm following a different
15   obsession.

vista: a view across a great distance
Papay: one of the Orkney Islands

1 How do I identify and compare relevant ideas and perspectives?

Before you can develop your comparison of two writers' ideas and perspectives, you need to compare:

- what they are writing about: the **topic** of their text
- the writer's **ideas and opinions** about the topic of their text
- the writers' **intentions**: the impact they want to have on the reader.

1 Complete the sentences below to summarise the key similarities and differences in the two texts, the writers' ideas and perspectives, and their intentions.

A. Comparing topics

Both texts are about ....

....

However in Text 1 ....

....

....

whereas in Text 2 ....

....

....

B. Comparing ideas and opinions

Both writers think that ....

....

However in Text 1 ....

....

....

whereas in Text 2 ....

....

....

C. Comparing intentions

Both writers want their readers to ....

....

However in Text 1 ....

....

....

whereas in Text 2 ....

....

....

② How do I develop my comparison of ideas and perspectives?

To develop your comparison of the writer's ideas and perspectives, you need to explore **how** they are conveyed.

① Look closely at four key quotations from **Text 1** and from **Text 2** below.

Text 1: The Lost Continent

A.
> a deep, inexpressible awe that anything on this earth could be so vast, so beautiful

B.
> I was a particularly talkative and obnoxious child, but it stopped me cold.

C.
> It is ten miles across, a mile deep, 180 miles long.

D.
> It looks like an old shoelace.

Text 2: The Outrun

A.
> I… say, 'Bloody hell,' out loud.

B.
> white 'searchlights' …dancing waves …blood red blooms

C.
> an unusual kind of light, the eerie glow of a floodlit stadium or a picnic eaten in car headlights

D.
> tonight I'm wild on Northern Lights. I'm following a different obsession.

Can you spot any similarities or differences in the way that each writer conveys their ideas and perspectives in the quotations above?

a Circle Ⓐ **one** of the boxed words in each of the sentences below to sum up any similarities or differences you have spotted.

			Text 1 Quote	Text 2 Quote
Both	One	of the writers describe(s) their feelings.		
Both	One	of the writers use(s) a comparison.		
Both	One	of the writers use(s) visual description.		
Both	One	of the writers use(s) facts and statistics.		

b Choose a quote from each of the texts above as evidence to support your answers. Write 🖉 the letter of your chosen quotations at the end of each sentence.

③ How do I structure my comparison?

When you write a comparison of the writers' ideas and perspectives in two texts, you need to:
- identify a similarity or difference in the writers' ideas and perspectives

and/or
- identify a similarity or difference in the ways in which they convey them

and
- closely analyse how they have used language and structure to convey them.

For more help with commenting on language and structure, see Units 3, 4 and 5.

① Look at the sentences below. They are from one paragraph of a student's response to this exam-style question.

Exam-style question

Compare how the writers of Text 1 and Text 2 present their ideas and perspectives about the natural world. Support your answer with detailed reference to the texts.

(14 marks)

Which of the sentences would you include in a paragraph comparing the two texts? Tick ✓ them.

Writing about both texts

A. | Both writers describe the natural world and express the great impact that it has on them. | ☐ ☐

B. | Text 1 explains how the Canyon was created but Text 2 does not explain how the Northern Lights are made. | ☐ ☐

C. | The writer of Text 2 does not describe her reaction so clearly or in as much detail as the writer of Text 1. | ☐ ☐

Writing about Text 1

D. | In Text 1, the writer describes 'a deep, inexpressible awe that anything on this earth could be so vast, so beautiful, so silent.' | ☐ ☐

E. | He repeats the word 'so' and uses a series of adjectives to highlight how powerful and impressive he finds the Grand Canyon. | ☐ ☐

F. | He uses lots of statistics, for example, 'ten miles across, a mile deep, 180 miles long'. | ☐ ☐

Writing about Text 2

G. | The writer of Text 2 describes how 'the whole sky is alive with shapes'. | ☐ ☐

H. | She sums up her amazement by saying that the lights made her swear. | ☐ ☐

I. | This suggests she cannot explain in words the effect that the lights have on her, which makes them seem all the more amazing. | ☐ ☐

② Number ✏ the sentences you have ticked to show how you would sequence them in a paragraph.

Comparing ideas and perspectives

An effective comparison focuses on the writers' ideas and perspectives **and** how they are conveyed.

Look at this exam-style question you saw at the start of the unit.

> **Exam-style question**
>
> Compare how the writers of Text 1 and Text 2 present their ideas and perspectives about the natural world.
>
> Support your answer with detailed references to the texts. (14 marks)

1 Now look at the paragraph below, written by a student in response to this exam-style question.

> Both writers try to describe the experience of seeing an amazing natural phenomenon: the Grand Canyon in Text 1 and the Northern Lights in Text 2. The writer of Text 1 compares the 300 foot wide Colorado River to 'an old shoelace' as you look down on it from the top of the Grand Canyon. This comparison emphasises how massive and amazing the Canyon is. The writer of Text 2 compares the Northern Lights to 'the eerie glow of a floodlit stadium or a picnic eaten in car headlights'. This shows how strange and unnatural the light of the Northern Lights is. Both writers use familiar, everyday objects and experiences to help the reader visualise unfamiliar and incredible wonders of the natural world.

a Annotate the paragraph, underlining Ⓐ and labelling 🖉 where in the paragraph this student has achieved the key features noted below.

   A. Identifies a similarity or difference in the two writers' ideas and perspectives.

   B. Supports with a quotation or textual reference from Text 1.

   C. Analyses the impact of the quotation from Text 1.

   D. Supports with a quotation or textual reference from Text 2.

   E. Analyses the impact of the quotation from Text 2.

   F. Compares how the two writers have conveyed their ideas and perspectives and/or compares the impact of the writers' choices on the reader.

b How could this student improve the paragraph above? Write 🖉 a sentence or two summarising your ideas.

....

....

....

....

....

Your turn!

You are now going to write your own response to the exam-style question.

> **Exam-style question**
>
> Compare how the writers of Text 1 and Text 2 present their ideas and perspectives about the natural world.
>
> Support your answer with detailed references to the texts.
>
> (14 marks)

(1) You should spend 20–25 minutes on this kind of question, so should aim to write three or four paragraphs. Use the space below to plan three paragraphs. ✎

	Similarity or difference	Text 1: Evidence	Text 2: Evidence
1			
2			
3			

(2) Now write ✎ your response to the exam-style question above on paper.

Review your skills

Check up

Review your response to the exam-style question on page 63. Tick ✓ the column to show how well you think you have done each of the following.

	Not quite ✓	Nearly there ✓	Got it! ✓
identified and compared similarities and differences in the writers' ideas and perspectives	☐	☐	☐
analysed and compared how the writers convey their ideas and perspectives	☐	☐	☐
structured a comparison of the writers' ideas and perspectives	☐	☐	☐

Need more practice?

Need more practice? Here is another exam-style question, this time relating to Text 2 on page 74: an extract from Maya Angelou's autobiography, *I Know Why The Caged Bird Sings*, published in 1969 and Text 3 on page 75: *A Back Seat Education*, a newspaper article published in 2016. You'll find some suggested points to refer to in the Answers section.

Exam-style question

Compare how the writers of Text 1 and Text 2 present their ideas and perspectives about young people.

Support your answer with detailed references to the texts.

(14 marks)

How confident do you feel about each of these **skills?** Colour ✏ in the bars.

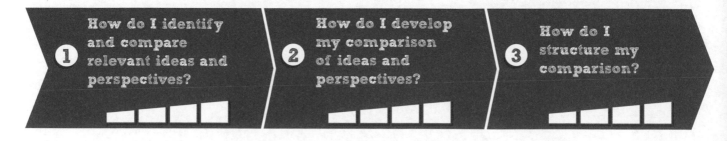

1 How do I identify and compare relevant ideas and perspectives?

2 How do I develop my comparison of ideas and perspectives?

3 How do I structure my comparison?

⑨ Expressing your ideas clearly and precisely

This unit will help you learn how to express your ideas clearly and precisely. The skills you will build are to:

- select vocabulary to express your ideas precisely
- link your ideas to express them clearly
- extend your sentences to develop ideas more fully.

In the exam you will face questions like the one below. This is about the text on page 66. At the end of the unit you will write your own response to this question.

Exam-style question

In this extract, there is an attempt to show the narrator's fear.

Evaluate how successfully this is achieved.

Support your views with detailed reference to the text.

(15 marks)

Before you tackle the question you will work through three key questions in the **skills boosts** to help you express your ideas clearly and precisely.

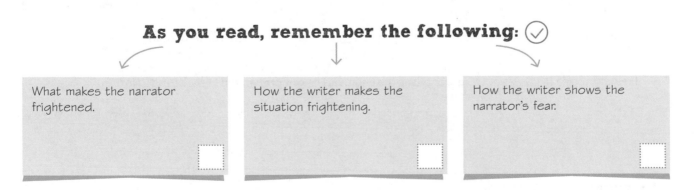

1 How do I choose vocabulary which expresses my ideas precisely?

2 How can I link my ideas to express them more clearly?

3 How can I extend my sentences to develop my ideas more fully?

Read the extract on page 66 from *Great Expectations* by Charles Dickens, published in 1861. You will tackle a 19th century fiction extract in the Reading section of your Paper 1 exam.

As you read, remember the following: ⊘

What makes the narrator frightened.	How the writer makes the situation frightening.	How the writer shows the narrator's fear.

In the decades since Miss Havisham's fiancé failed to turn up for their wedding, she has not removed her wedding dress or left her house. In this extract the narrator, a young boy named Pip, has come to Miss Havisham's house to play with her adopted daughter.

Text 1 Great Expectations, Charles Dickens

I knocked, and was told from within to enter. I entered, therefore, and found myself in a pretty large room, well lighted with wax candles. No glimpse of daylight was to be seen in it. It was a dressing-room, as I supposed from the furniture, though much of it was of forms and uses then quite unknown to me. But prominent in it was a draped table with a gilded looking-glass, and that I made out at first sight to be a fine lady's dressing-table.

5 Whether I should have made out this object so soon if there had been no fine lady sitting at it, I cannot say. In an arm-chair, with an elbow resting on the table and her head leaning on that hand, sat the strangest lady I have ever seen, or shall ever see.

She was dressed in rich materials,—satins, and lace, and silks,—all of white. Her shoes were white. And she had a long white veil **dependent** from her hair, and she had bridal flowers in her hair, but her hair was white. Some

10 bright jewels sparkled on her neck and on her hands, and some other jewels lay sparkling on the table. Dresses, less splendid than the dress she wore, and half-packed trunks, were scattered about. She had not quite finished dressing, for she had but one shoe on,—the other was on the table near her hand,—her veil was but half arranged, her watch and chain were not put on, and some lace for her bosom lay with those trinkets, and with her handkerchief, and gloves, and some flowers, and a Prayer-Book all confusedly heaped about the looking-glass.

15 It was not in the first few moments that I saw all these things, though I saw more of them in the first moments than might be supposed. But I saw that everything within my view which ought to be white, had been white long ago, and had lost its lustre and was faded and yellow. I saw that the bride within the bridal dress had withered like the dress, and like the flowers, and had no brightness left but the brightness of her sunken eyes. I saw that the dress had been put upon the rounded figure of a young woman, and that the figure upon which it now hung loose

20 had shrunk to skin and bone. Once, I had been taken to see some ghastly waxwork at the Fair, representing I know not what impossible personage lying in state. Once, I had been taken to one of our old **marsh churches** to see a skeleton in the ashes of a rich dress that had been dug out of a vault under the church pavement. Now, waxwork and skeleton seemed to have dark eyes that moved and looked at me. I should have cried out, if I could.

"Who is it?" said the lady at the table.

25 "Pip, ma'am."

"Pip?"

"Mr. Pumblechook's boy, ma'am. Come—to play."

"Come nearer; let me look at you. Come close."

It was when I stood before her, avoiding her eyes, that I took note of the surrounding objects in detail, and saw

30 that her watch had stopped at twenty minutes to nine, and that a clock in the room had stopped at twenty minutes to nine.

"Look at me," said Miss Havisham. "You are not afraid of a woman who has never seen the sun since you were born?"

I regret to state that I was not afraid of telling the enormous lie **comprehended** in the answer "No."

dependent: attached to, hanging
marsh churches: churches in the marshlands of Kent where the novel is set
comprehended: contained

1 How do I choose vocabulary which expresses my ideas precisely?

When writing about a text, you need to choose vocabulary which is appropriately formal and expresses your ideas as clearly and precisely as possible.

① Look at some possible vocabulary choices to describe the narrator in the extract on page 66.

> In this extract the narrator is presented as

| scared ☐ | terrified ☐ | petrified ☐ | afraid ☐ | _____ ☐ |
| anxious ☐ | alarmed ☐ | upset ☐ | worried ☐ | _____ ☐ |

a Add ✐ two more possible vocabulary choices in the blank spaces.

b Which vocabulary choice describes your impression of the narrator most accurately? Tick ✓ it.

c Write ✐ a sentence explaining your choice.

....

....

② Look at this quotation.

> "Look at me," said Miss Havisham. "You are not afraid of a woman who has never seen the sun since you were born?"

Now look at the analysis of this quotation and some possible vocabulary choices you could use to complete it. Choose the clearest, most precise vocabulary choices to fill the blanks.

In the command to 'Look at me',

and the question that follows,

| suggests
implies
creates the impression
makes me think
means |

the writer .... that

Miss Havisham is ....

| both
neither
extremely
rather
slightly |

.... , ...

| bossy
grumpy
aggressive
angry
domineering |

| and
yet
or
nor
but |

| unsettling
weird
disturbing
odd
eccentric |

③ Look at the description of Miss Havisham in the third paragraph of the extract.

a Note down ✐ **four** possible vocabulary choices to describe her.

.... ☐   .... ☐   .... ☐   .... ☐

b Tick ✓ the **two** vocabulary choices that you think are most precise and accurate.

Unit 9 Expressing your ideas clearly and precisely 67

2 How can I link my ideas to express them more clearly?

Conjunctions can link your ideas, making them more clearly and fluently expressed.

Coordinating conjunctions, such as:

| and | but | or | so |

can join related or contrasting ideas.

Subordinating conjunctions express more complex connections such as:

- an explanation e.g. | because | in order to |
- a condition e.g. | if | unless |
- a comparison e.g. | although | whereas |
- a sequence e.g. | when | before | until |

① Compare these sentences from student answer A with single sentences B and C.

A. | Pip is clearly frightened. | | He does not admit it to Miss Havisham. | | ☐ |

B. | Pip is clearly frightened, | | but | | he does not admit it to Miss Havisham. | | ☐ |

C. | Although | | Pip is clearly frightened, | | he does not admit it to Miss Havisham. | | ☐ |

a Which version is expressed most clearly and fluently? Tick ✓ it.

b Write ✐ a sentence explaining your choice.

....

....

② Rewrite ✐ the pairs of sentences below into single sentences using a conjunction to make each one's meaning clearer and its expression more fluent. Remember to adjust the punctuation.

A. The narrator suggests Miss Havisham is dying and decaying. He describes her as 'withered'.

....

....

B. Pip is completely silent. He answers Miss Havisham's questions at the end of the extract.

....

....

....

C. Pip is obviously terrified of Miss Havisham. He compares her to a waxwork and a skeleton.

....

....

....

③ How can I extend my sentences to develop my ideas more fully?

You can extend your sentences by linking related ideas in a number of different ways.

One way is to use a present participle: the verb form that ends in *-ing*. For example:

The writer creates a sense of fear in Pip's description of Miss Havisham.	+	He describes her as 'shrunk to skin and bone.'	=	The writer creates a sense of fear in Pip's description of Miss Havisham
				describing
				her as 'shrunk to skin and bone.'

The present participle 'describing' clearly and fluently links these two points.

① Present participles are the form of a verb that ends in *-ing*. Complete 🖉 the table below, adding the present participles of these three verbs. The first one has been done to help you.

Verb	Present participle
build	*building*
wear	
sit	
hide	

② Rewrite 🖉 the two sentences below, using a present participle to create a single sentence.

| The narrator gives a long description of Miss Havisham's strange appearance. | +

| It builds up to the short, dramatic sentence, 'I should have cried out, if I could.' | =

....

....

....

....

③ You can add a range of detailed information to sentences using a number of present participles. Use present participles to link these **four** ideas into a single sentence. Write 🖉 your sentence below.

| The image of Miss Havisham is of a faded, almost decaying woman. |

| She wears a faded wedding dress. | | She sits in her candle-lit dressing room. |

| She hides from the outside world. |

....

....

....

....

....

Expressing your ideas clearly and precisely

To express your ideas as clearly and precisely as possible, you need to think about:

- selecting the most precise vocabulary
- linking and extending your ideas using conjunctions and/or present participles.

Now look at this exam-style question you saw at the start of the unit.

Exam-style question

In this extract, there is an attempt to show the narrator's fear.

Evaluate how successfully this is achieved.

Support your views with detailed reference to the text.

(15 marks)

(1) Look at a short paragraph from one student's response to the task.

> The narrator's description gives a feeling of the fear he has for Miss Havisham. He describes her as a waxwork and a skeleton 'with dark eyes that moved and looked at me.' This is a scary image. It suggests she is dead and not human. It also suggests she is watching him carefully. It creates the feeling that he is in danger.

a Underline Ⓐ three examples of vocabulary which could be more precise.

b Note 🖉 down in the margin **at least three** alternative vocabulary choices for each one.

c Mark 🖉 any of the sentences which you feel should be linked or developed to improve the clarity and precision of the writing.

d Write 🖉 an improved version of this paragraph, either by adjusting the text above or by re-writing it in the space below or on paper.

Your turn!

You are now going to write just **one** paragraph in response to this exam-style question.

Exam-style question

In this extract, there is an attempt to show the narrator's fear.

Evaluate how successfully this is achieved.

Support your views with detailed reference to the text. **(15 marks)**

In your exam, you should spend around 20–25 minutes on this type of question and write four or five paragraphs. However, you are now going to write just **one** paragraph. This will allow you to focus more closely on expressing your ideas as clearly and precisely as possible.

(1) Look at some of the features of the extract on page 66 which contribute to showing the narrator's fear:

Feature	Quotation
The narrator describes Miss Havisham: ☐	the bride within the bridal dress had withered like the dress
	the dress had been put upon the rounded figure of a young woman, and that the figure upon which it now hung loose had shrunk to skin and bone.
The narrator compares Miss Havisham to: ☐	some ghastly waxwork at the Fair
	a skeleton in the ashes of a rich dress that had been dug out of a vault
The narrator describes how Miss Havisham behaves and what she says: ☐	waxwork and skeleton seemed to have dark eyes that moved and looked at me.
	"Come nearer; let me look at you. Come close."
	"Look at me," said Miss Havisham. "You are not afraid of a woman who has never seen the sun since you were born?"
The narrator describes his feelings: ☐	I should have cried out, if I could.

a Choose **one** ✓ of the features above which you can explore in your response to the exam-style question.

b Use your chosen feature and at least one quotation to write ✐ a paragraph in response to the exam-style question on paper. Remember to:

- choose your vocabulary carefully
- think about ways in which you can link your ideas to express them clearly and precisely.

Review your skills

Check up

Review your response to the exam-style question on page 71. Tick ⊘ the column to show how well you think you have done each of the following.

	Not quite ⊘	Nearly there ⊘	Got it! ⊘
selected precise vocabulary	☐	☐	☐
linked ideas clearly and precisely with conjunctions	☐	☐	☐
linked ideas clearly and precisely with present participles	☐	☐	☐

Look over all of your work in this unit. Note down ✎ the three most important things to remember when trying to express your ideas as clearly and precisely as possible.

1. ....

2. ....

3. ....

Need more practice?

You can EITHER:

① Look again at your paragraph written in response to the exam-style question on page 71. Re-write it ✎, experimenting with different vocabulary choices and sentence structures, linking your ideas in different ways. Which are most effective in expressing your ideas clearly and precisely?

AND/OR

② Choose a **second** point from the suggestions on page 71. Write ✎ a further paragraph in response to the exam-style question, focusing closely on your vocabulary choice and sentence structures.

How confident do you feel about each of these **skills?** Colour ✎ in the bars.

① How do I choose vocabulary which expresses my ideas precisely? ☐☐☐☐

② How can I link my ideas to express them more clearly? ☐☐☐☐

③ How can I extend my sentences to develop my ideas more fully? ☐☐☐☐

More practice texts

Sherlock Holmes and his friend and associate, Dr Watson, are travelling through Switzerland, hunting down the criminal mastermind, Professor Moriarty. In this extract, they pass the Reichenbach Falls — one of the highest, and most dramatic waterfalls in the Alps.

Text 1: The Final Problem, Arthur Conan Doyle, 1893

It is indeed, a fearful place. The torrent, swollen by the melting snow, plunges into a tremendous abyss, from which the spray rolls up like the smoke from a burning house. The shaft into which the river hurls itself is an immense chasm, lined by glistening coal-black rock, and narrowing into a creaming, boiling pit of incalculable depth, which brims over and shoots the stream onward over its jagged lip. The long sweep of green water roaring forever down, and the thick flickering curtain of spray hissing forever upward, turn a man giddy with their constant whirl and clamor. We stood near the edge peering down at the gleam of the breaking water far below us against the black rocks, and listening to the half-human shout which came booming up with the spray out of the abyss.

The path has been cut half-way round the fall to afford a complete view, but it ends abruptly, and the traveler has to return as he came. We had turned to do so, when we saw a Swiss lad come running along it with a letter in his hand. It bore the mark of the hotel which we had just left, and was addressed to me by the landlord. It appeared that within a very few minutes of our leaving, an English lady had arrived who was in the last stage of **consumption**. It was thought that she could hardly live a few hours, but it would be a great consolation to her to see an English doctor, and, if I would only return, etc

The appeal was one which could not be ignored. My friend would stay some little time at the fall, he said, and would then walk slowly over the hill to Rosenlaui, where I was to rejoin him in the evening. As I turned away I saw Holmes, with his back against a rock and his arms folded, gazing down at the rush of the waters. It was the last that I was ever destined to see of him in this world.

It may have been a little over an hour before I reached Meiringen. Old Steiler was standing at the porch of his hotel.

"Well," said I, as I came hurrying up, "I trust that she is no worse?"

A look of surprise passed over his face, and at the first quiver of his eyebrows my heart turned to lead in my breast.

"You did not write this?" I said, pulling the letter from my pocket. "There is no sick Englishwoman in the hotel?"

"Certainly not!" he cried. "But it has the hotel mark upon it! Ha, it must have been written by that tall Englishman who came in after you had gone. He said—"

But I waited for none of the landlord's explanations. In a tingle of fear I was already running down the village street, and making for the path which I had so lately descended. It had taken me an hour to come down. For all my efforts two more had passed before I found myself at the fall of Reichenbach once more. There was Holmes's **Alpine-stock** still leaning against the rock by which I had left him. But there was no sign of him, and it was in vain that I shouted. My only answer was my own voice reverberating in a rolling echo from the cliffs around me.

consumption: a disease of the lungs, now known as tuberculosis
Alpine-stock: a walking stick used by walkers and hikers.

Maya Angelou grew up with her grandmother, Momma, her Uncle Willie and her brother, Bailey. In this extract, Bailey has not come home. The writer and her grandmother go out looking for him.

Text 2: I Know Why The Caged Bird Sings, Maya Angelou, 1969

It was darker in the road than I'd thought it would be. Momma swung the flashlight's arc over the path and weeds and scary tree trunks. The night suddenly became enemy territory, and I knew that if my brother was lost in this land he was forever lost. He was eleven and very smart, that I granted, but after all he was so small. The **Bluebeards** and tigers and Rippers could eat him up before he could scream for help.

Momma told me to take the light and she reached for my hand. Her voice came from a high hill above me and in the dark my hand was enclosed in hers. I loved her with a rush. She said nothing–no "Don't worry" or "Don't get tender-hearted." Just the gentle pressure of her rough hand conveyed her own concern and assurance to me.

We passed houses which I knew well by daylight but couldn't recollect in the swarthy gloom.

"Evening, Miz Jenkins." Walking and pulling me along.

"Sister Henderson? Anything wrong?" That was from an outline blacker than the night.

"No, ma'am. Not a thing. Bless the Lord." By the time she finished speaking we had left the worried neighbors far behind.

Mr. Willie Williams' Do Drop Inn was bright with furry red lights in the distance and the pond's fishy smell enveloped us. Momma's hand tightened and let go, and I saw the small figure plodding along, tired and oldmannish. Hands in his pockets and head bent, he walked like a man trudging up the hill behind a coffin.

"Bailey." It jumped out as Momma said, "Ju," and I started to run, but her hand caught mine again and became a vise. I pulled, but she yanked me back to her side. "We'll walk, just like we been walking, young lady." There was no chance to warn Bailey that he was dangerously late, that everybody had been worried and that he should create a good lie or, better, a great one.

Momma said, "Bailey, Junior," and he looked up without surprise. "You know it's night and you just now getting home?"

"Yes, ma'am." He was empty. Where was his alibi? "What you been doing?"

"Nothing."

"That's all you got to say?"

"Yes, ma'am."

"All right, young man. We'll see when you get home." She had turned me loose, so I made a grab for Bailey's hand, but he snatched it away. I said, "Hey, Bail," hoping to remind him that I was his sister and his only friend, but he grumbled something like "Leave me alone."

Momma didn't turn on the flashlight on the way back, nor did she answer the questioning Good evenings that floated around us as we passed the darkened houses.

I was confused and frightened. He was going to get a whipping and maybe he had done something terrible. If he couldn't talk to me it must have been serious. But there was no air of spent revelry about him. He just seemed sad. I didn't know what to think.

Uncle Willie said, "Getting too big for your britches, huh? You can't come home. You want to worry your grandmother to death?" Bailey was so far away he was beyond fear. Uncle Willie had a leather belt in his good hand but Bailey didn't notice or didn't care.

Bluebeard: a character in a folk tale who repeatedly marries then murders his wives.

Author Marianne Levy describes her journey on a school bus to see whether things had changed in the two decades since she last went on a school bus.

Text 3: A Back Seat Education, Marianne Levy, 2016

"I only like him about 30 per cent now. Which is way down from before, when I liked him 100 per cent."

"That's so many per cent, Ruby."

"I know."

Ever wondered what happens after you've dropped your teenager at the bus stop? As the nation's children returned for the January term, I decided to find out, and now I'm sitting on the back seat with the 4pm crowd, right between Ruby and her friend, my head swivelling to catch their words over the growl of the engine. I'm the most obvious undercover reporter ever. But I'm not wearing school uniform, and so, as far as they're concerned, I'm completely invisible.

A lot has happened in the couple of decades since I took the bus to school. But it's good to know that some things haven't really changed.

Though I am currently juddering across north London, my journey once took me from Chelmsford to Colchester and back. It was a 50-mile round trip. And it made *Lord of the Flies* look like a spa break. So when I was searching for a scary landscape into which to plunge the heroine of my new teen-fiction novel, there was no need to conjure up a vampire-ridden dystopia; I just had to travel back 20 years in my own head.

The discussion turns to whether or not Ali's shoes are Air Max ("Obviously they are not," says Ruby), and as we turn a corner, I stagger down towards the front to check in on a pair of tiny boys, apple-cheeked angels in blazers. The more cherubic of the two is spewing forth a stream of swearwords. His friend responds by bashing him over the head with a violin case. It's all reassuringly familiar, although I'm worried for the violin.

In my days of getting the bus, I wouldn't have given the safety of musical instruments a second thought; my entire focus was on self-preservation. Culled from four very different schools and trapped together for around 15 hours every week, we formed a strange, uneasy society.

There were adults, of course, but they ignored us. The bus driver, occasionally called upon to intervene after a particularly brutal fight, would inevitably refuse to get involved, saying gloomily (and probably correctly), "I'm not paid enough for this."

There were moments of genuine danger, too: the night my friend crossed in front of the bus and bounced off a Volvo through a lane of fast traffic; the time the sunroof caught a branch and flew off, leaving a square of night sky pouring cold air down on to our surprised heads.

Whole lifetimes' worth of social interaction could be condensed into a single journey; wars fought, bonds forged and loves lost while the double-decker idled in traffic on the Kelvedon slip road.

Do I miss it? Maybe, just a little. It was exhausting, the constant attack and defence, the emotional energy we'd expend on the most trivial arguments, the way any foodstuff might be turned into a missile. But then there were the frosty mornings when we'd send our breath up in warm white plumes and pretend we were holding cigarettes, the secrets shared over a flaking Curly Wurly as the top deck emptied, the friendships so intense they burned.

Back in London, the girls barge past me, and, as though to drive the point home, one actually stands on my foot as she reaches for the bell.

"See ya, Rubes," says her friend, swinging off on to the pavement. And Ruby settles down into her seat, pops her headphones into her ears, and flashes me a tiny, satisfied smile.

Answers

Unit 1

Page 3

(1) (a) i. fan-light (line 2): a window above a door, shaped like a fan.

ii. trifle (line 6): a little, slightly.

iii. neckerchief (line 7): a piece of cloth worn around the neck.

iv. scholastic (line 7): academic, related to education.

v. the Beggar's Petition in printed calico (line 35): a popular poem, printed on cloth.

(2) e.g. This is a fiction text about the headteacher of a school waiting for new pupils. The writer presents the headteacher as a bad tempered, ruthless and violent villain and encourages the reader's sympathy for his victims.

Page 4

(1) Paragraph 1: Squeers' physical appearance.

Paragraph 2: A description of the coffee-room and a small boy.

Paragraphs 3–5: Squeers is angry because no parents have come to him.

Paragraphs 6–end: Squeers takes his temper out on the boy.

(2) (a) e.g. The boy 'glanced timidly at the schoolmaster'.

(b) e.g. 'looking sulkily', 'much vexed'.

Page 5

(1) The text aims to engage the reader's interest, introduce the character of Squeers, creating sympathy for the boy and antipathy for Squeers.

(2) (b) Throughout the extract, Squeers is presented in a negative light: he looks 'villainous', is bad-tempered ('much vexed') and considers his pupils as a source of money ('ten twenties is two hundred pound') and an irritation on which to vent his temper ('boxed his ears'). The reader's sympathy is clearly directed towards his victim, the vulnerable 'diminutive boy'.

Page 6

The response does not answer the question. It is broadly focused on the character of Squeers, not on his interest in money. A more effective response would link Squeers' bad temper to the calculations he makes, valuing each prospective pupil at twenty pounds per year.

Page 7

(1) 'a very sinister appearance', 'his expression bordered closely on the villainous'.

(2) 'what does it all mean?'

Page 8

Q	I Know Why The Caged Bird Sings
	1. From lines 1–5, identify **one** reason that the writer is worried about her brother.
	(1 mark)
	2. From lines 15–28, give **two** examples that suggest Bailey is unhappy. [from 'Mr Willie Williams...' to '"Yes, ma'am."') **(2 marks)**
A	1. He is lost; he is very small; the outside world is a dangerous place.
	2. 'plodding along... head bent... trudging ... behind a coffin... He was empty.'

Unit 2

Page 11

(1) All are potentially valid choices.

Page 12

(1) B. e.g. 'stabbed... shaken... white-hot' all suggest the power and violence of the attack; 'sparkling', in contrast, suggests the beauty of the scene, a response which the writer develops further towards the end of the article.

C. The sentence is structured as a list, suggesting the range and variety of impacts the bombing has had.

D. The writer's choices suggest the intention to convey the chaos and devastation of attack but also hints at feelings of awe and excitement.

Page 13

(1)(2) A is the longest response, but the least developed; B gives limited comment on word choice; C gives a detailed and specific comment on word and sentence structure choice so offers the most developed analysis.

(3) May comment on the onomatopoeia of 'boom, crump', the word choice 'tearing' to suggest violence, the short final sentence building tension as the planes and the bombing approach.

Page 14

quotation from the text	'the monstrous loveliness of that one single view of London'.
comments on vocabulary and/or sentence structure choices	The adjective 'monstrous' presents the bombers as monsters and the people of London as their helpless victims but 'loveliness' suggests that the burning city is a beautiful sight.
comments precisely on the impact of these choices on readers	The writer's reaction to the attack is very surprising and even shocking for readers... These mixed emotions of horror, excitement and beauty show what a strange and terrible experience it was.
use key words from the question	The vocabulary in this sentence is one of the most engaging and interesting parts of the text.

2. The paragraph is structured: explain-evidence-point-explain. The key idea to explore is that, while P/E/E can support students in developing their analytical skills, slavishly following it can limit analysis and, therefore, achievement.

Page 16

Q	The Final Problem
	In lines 1 to 8, how does the writer use language and structure to show the impact of the Reichenbach Falls on the narrator?
	Support your views with reference to the text.
	(6 marks)
A	Language
	Adjective choices emphasise the scale of the Falls: 'tremendous... immense... incalculable.'
	Dramatic comparisons suggest danger: 'a burning house... a creaming, boiling pit'.
	Structure
	A short, emphatic sentence 'It is indeed, a fearful place.' summarises the narrator's response.
	Several multiple clause sentences build detail and reflect the scale and power of the Falls.

Unit 3

Page 19

1. Frightened, upset.
2. 2, 3, 5 and 6 suggest fear.
3. a bewilderment, terror, towered, wept, knife-edged, wicked.
4. • 'I wept' because it suggests the narrator is frightened and upset.
   • 'didn't know where to move' because it suggests the narrator is paralysed with fear.
   • 'knife-edged, dark, and a wicked green' because it suggests he is even frightened of the grass.
   • 'screaming' because it suggests he is frightened of the birds and the noises they make.

Page 20

1. e.g. frightened, intimidated, threatened, abandoned.
2. a sympathy
   b 'lost', 'sun hit me smartly on the face, like a bully'
3. a b e.g. 'howled' shows he is upset; 'did not expect to be found again' suggests he feels abandoned.

Page 21

1. a b c Suggests a distressed, wild animal; suggests narrator is distressed and wild with fear, encouraging the reader to understand how upset he is and therefore feel sympathy for him.
2. a b Suggests the narrator is a victim of the sun's bullying bright light – more usually considered something positive - again creating sympathy.

Page 22

1. Analyse, language and structure, engage and interest readers, detailed reference.
2.

uses key words from the question	The writer engages the reader's interest... This language...
identifies the writer's intention	Creating sympathy for the narrator.
supported with evidence from the text	How upset and threatened the narrator feels... 'It was knife-edged, dark, and a wicked green'.
comments on connotations of language choices	The word 'knife-edged' makes it sound sharp and dangerous and threatening and the word 'wicked' makes it sound evil and like it is trying to harm him.
comments on how this helps to achieve the writer's intention	This language makes us feel sorry for the narrator because he is so young and he thinks he is in serious danger.

Page 24

Q	The Final Problem
	How does the writer use language and structure to show Watson's reaction to being tricked? (6 marks)
A	Language
	The metaphor 'turned to lead' implies the narrator's shock and dismay.
	The narrator describes his 'fear' as a physical 'tingle' making it more vivid.
	The narrator shouts 'in vain' suggesting his increasing desperation.
	Structure
	Short paragraphs of dialogue increase the pace of the text as the narrator first realises he has been tricked.
	Short sentences in the final longer paragraph suggest the narrator's frantic reaction.

Unit 4

Page 27

1. To show how ordinary people who overcome adversity can inspire people and change their attitudes to disability.

2. All paragraphs contribute to the writer's intention.

3. The text features:
   - a thought provoking introduction
   - a powerful conclusion
   - the main body of the article structured as a chronological story
   - quotes.

4. The first three paragraphs focus on celebrities to highlight how they can have an impact on our lives; a point which the concluding three paragraphs refer to in order to highlight the impact that ordinary people can have.

5. The writer structures key moments from Andrea Annear's life as a chronological narrative.

6. While the introduction and conclusion make an engaging, interesting point, it could be argued that the main interest and engagement of the article comes from the focus on Andrea Annear's relationship with her husband, the attitudes that prevented their marriage, and how they overcame them, effectively presenting her life as a romantic tale with a happy ending.

Page 28

1. e.g.

   A/C 'Now consider the case of Andrea Annear.'

   B 'She was born in about 1969 with Down's Syndrome, a condition which gave her slowed development, distinctive facial features, a weak heart and a lowered IQ.'

   D. Eventually, after much persuasion, they got their wish.

2. **a** **b** The original is structured as two short sentences, not one longer sentence, with adverbials fronted ('Without each other... Together...'), delaying key information dramatically to the end of the sentence. The parallel structure of the two sentences adds further impact.

Page 29

1. e.g.
   - Sentence A: 'Now consider the case of Andrea Annear.' A short sentence, adding emphasis to contrast celebrities and Andrea Annear, emphasising that ordinary people can inspire us.
   - Sentence B: 'She was born in about 1969 with Down's Syndrome, a condition which gave her slowed development, distinctive facial features, a weak heart and a lowered IQ.' A longer sentence, providing descriptive detail, highlighting what Andrea had to overcome.
   - Sentence F: 'Eventually, after much persuasion, they got their wish.' A short sentence, fronted with 'eventually' to highlight how long they had to wait, and delaying key information to the end of the sentence to build tension. Emphatically highlights what Andrea achieved, engaging the reader in Andrea's story.

Page 30

1. Analyse, writer, language, structure, interest, engage, readers, detailed reference.

2. Student B's response is the most effective. It features the most detailed analysis, clearly focused on the exam-style question.

Page 32

Q	A Back Seat education
	Analyse how the writer uses language and structure to interest and engage readers.
	Support your views with detailed reference to the text. (15 marks)
A	**Language**
	The writer uses humorous comparisons 'it made Lord of the Flies look like a spa break.'
	The writer creates a humorous and vivid description by contrasting the appearance of 'apple-cheeked angels' with the reality of one 'spewing forth a stream of swearwords' while another is 'bashing him over the head'.
	Detailed descriptive language builds vivid, evocative images of e.g. 'a square of night sky pouring cold air down on to our surprised heads', 'we'd send our breath up in warm white plumes and pretend we were holding cigarettes'.
	Structure
	The writer compares her personal childhood experience of the school bus with those of today's students to create a more developed account.
	The writer engages readers with humorous dialogue at the start of the article.
	The writer engages readers with a rhetorical question: 'Ever wondered what happens after you've dropped your teenager at the bus stop?'

Unit 5

Page 35

1.

A. e.g. 'slog' emphasising hard, gruelling work; final emphatic clause of sentence delayed and emphasised by adverbials 'all over the country... once again...' highlighting the scale and frequency of the situation.

B. List structure emphasises the variety of pain and suffering students must endure, highlighted by emotive, dramatic language choices e.g. 'cramping... coldly sweating...'.

C. Short emphatic sentences and repetition highlight the importance of exams.

D. Listed positive adjectives ('brilliant, concise, exciting') highlight a positive attitude to a difficult experience, signalled by the contrasting conjunction 'But', emphatically positioned as a sentence start.

Page 36

1. All are relevant and arguable.

2. **a** Highlights the reality of GCSEs.
   b All of the above.

(3) e.g. 'rush of adrenaline... tingling... cold wash of nerves...floods your stomach'.

The list cumulatively suggests and acknowledges the overwhelming emotional and physical experience of GCSEs.

Page 37

(1) G and H are least likely to form part of an effective analytical response.

(2) e.g. The writer uses lots of emotive language choices to describe the fear and anxiety of exams [D], <u>such as</u> 'the thump of your heart... the cold wash of nerves' [B]. However some of the strongest key points are delivered using very blunt, simple language. [C] <u>for example</u> 'Exams are not the time for peer pressure' [A]. The writer structures this point in a short sentence to add emphasis [E] effectively highlighting this as a key point which the reader should take to heart. [F]

Page 38

(1)

effective choice of quotation	'muffle the maddening soundtrack of ticking clocks, sniffing classmates, squeaking chairs and sobbing companions.'
identifies the writer's intention	The writer uses quite a lot of humour in the article.
analyses the impact of the writer's use of structure	Positioning the phrase 'sobbing companions' at the end of this long list adds to the humour because it's the most extreme example of what you might hear in an exam.

The response could include:
- more analysis of language choices, e.g. adjectives creating vivid aural imagery: 'maddening...sniffing... squeaking... sobbing...'
- reference to the use of humour to engage the reader's interest.

Page 39

Q	I Know Why The Caged Bird Sings
	Analyse how the writer uses language and structure to interest and engage readers.
	Support your views with detailed reference to the text. **(15 marks)**
A	Language
	Vocabulary choices in the opening description create an ominous mood, e.g. 'scary... enemy... bluebeards... rippers... tigers... scream'.
	Verbs used to describe how Mama holds the narrator's hand suggest her affection but also her dominance, e.g. 'enclosed... yanked... tightened'.
	Bailey is 'empty' and 'far away' suggesting something profound and serious has happened and so creating mystery and tension.
	Structure
	The writer delays the confrontation with Bailey to build tension.
	Short sentences of dialogue create a tense, awkward atmosphere.
	Bailey's very limited responses creates a sense of mystery.

Unit 6

Page 43

(1) All those listed; also perhaps to introduce character and setting.

(2) All, except 'Narrator has been hunting', arguably contribute to the sense of danger.

(3) e.g. The sense of danger grows throughout the extract as the writer establishes that the narrator is lost in a deserted landscape as night falls and the weather closes in.

Page 44

(1) e.g. concern, sympathy, shock.

(2) e.g.
- The exclamation creates shock as though the narrator is facing death as a very real possibility.
- 'shuddered' suggests the narrator's fear, arousing the reader's concern for his safety.
- The contrast creates sympathy as he may lose this life and his wife will be widowed.

Page 45

(1)(2) e.g.
- The writer's repetition of 'darken' and 'darkening' effectively suggests the approach of night mirroring and causing the narrator's hopes to fade, creating concern and sympathy in the reader.
- The writer's choice of the verb 'thickened' suggests the total darkness and the difficulty the narrator is in. The simple vocabulary choice and sentence structure bluntly emphasises the worsening situation, powerfully highlighting the growing sense of danger.
- The list of verbs describing the light flickering and approaching successfully creates tension, manipulating the reader as we wait to discover whether the narrator will be saved or whether his situation will worsen.

Page 46

focuses on a specific element of the text: the setting	At the beginning of the extract, the writer sets the scene.
uses key words from the question	She immediately creates a strong sense of danger.
evidence from the text	'a bleak wide moor'
comments on vocabulary and/or sentence structure choices	The adjectives 'bleak' and 'wide' powerfully suggest the narrator is in the middle of nowhere.
comments on how this helps to achieve the writer's intention	To dramatically emphasise the danger he is in.
comments on the impact of the text on the reader	This effectively encourages the reader to expect the narrator's situation to become even more dangerous.
uses evaluative language to comment on the writer's success in achieving her intention	

Page 48

Q	*The Final Problem*
	In this extract there is an attempt to create drama and tension.
	Evaluate how successfully this is achieved.
	Support your views with detailed reference to the text.
	(15 marks)
A	The description of the Falls creates a dramatic and dangerous mood.
	The dramatic call upon the narrator is still more dramatically revealed to be a trick.
	The final scene in the extract, as the narrator's shouts echo through the mountains, creates a dramatic and tense conclusion to the extract.

Unit 7

Page 51

Similarities include:

- both texts focus on elderly people
- both extracts recount humorous incidents.

Significant differences include:

- the narrator of Text 1 focuses on his grandfather's physical characteristics, while the narrator of Text 2 focuses on her mother's mental deterioration.
- in Text 1, the grandfather is the victim of a physical problem while in Text 2 the narrator's mother appears to share in the humour caused by her mental deterioration.

Page 52

Text 1

A: suggests the narrator does not have fond memories of his grandfather.

E/J: suggest the narrator sees his grandfather as a source of humour.

H: suggests the narrator has a rather heartless attitude to his grandfather's infirmity.

Text 2

B: suggests the narrator's sympathy for Janet.

D/F: suggest the narrator sees this incident as a source of humour.

G: again suggests humour but also fear for the impact which dementia will have on her mother in the future.

J: suggests the narrator is sharing the humour of the situation with her mother.

One of the narrators shows respect for the elderly: H, B.

Both of the narrators use humour: J, I.

Both of the narrators laughs at the elderly: J, G.

One of the narrators laughs with the elderly: K.

Page 53

A, B, E and F all focus on the narrator and so are relevant. C and D focus on details about the elderly people in the texts and are therefore not directly relevant to the exam-style question.

 e.g.

- Both narrators have chosen to write humorous stories about elderly relatives showing that they think the problems of old age can be entertaining.

- The narrators of both texts focus on the problems that elderly people experience. However, whereas the narrator in Text 1 is not very sympathetic to his grandfather's problems, the narrator in Text 2 writes about 'our future' suggesting she sees her mother's problems as something they will share.

Page 54

The response does achieve A and B, but not C: no evidence is provided to support the comment on Text 1.

Page 56

Q	Text 2: *I Know Why The Caged Bird Sings* and Text 3: *A Back Seat Education*
	The two texts show young people in different situations.
	What similarities do the young people share in these texts?
	Use evidence from both texts to support your answer. **(6 marks)**
A	Both texts show young people as vulnerable: in Text 2, the narrator is frightened for her brother and frightened of 'scary trees' and 'Bluebeards and tigers and Rippers'; in Text 3, the writer describes 'moments of genuine danger' such as when 'my friend crossed in front of the bus and bounced off a Volvo'.
	Both texts show young people disregarding adults: in Text 2, Bailey will not respond to Mama; in Text 3, the writer describes how she is 'completely invisible' to the young people on the bus, and how one student steps on her foot.
	Both texts show a difficult relationship between young people: in Text 2, Bailey will not respond to his sister; in Text 3, the writer describes 'wars fought, bonds forged and loves lost' on the school bus.

Unit 8

Page 59

 e.g.

A. Both texts are about wonders of the natural world. However, in Text 1 the writer focuses on the Grand Canyon, whereas in Text 2 the writer describes the Northern Lights.

B. Both writers think that their chosen topic is an incredible wonder of the natural world. However in Text 1 the writer concentrates on conveying the scale of the Grand Canyon whereas in Text 2 the writer tries to describe what the Northern Lights look and feel like.

C. Both writers want their readers to appreciate these natural phenomena. However, in Text 1, the writer wants the reader to appreciate the scale and impact of the Grand Canyon on everyone who sees it whereas in Text 2 the writer wants the reader to understand the impact that the Northern Lights had on her at this time in her life.

Page 60

(1) Both of the writers describe their feelings: A, B, E, H.

Both of the writers use a comparison: D, G.

Both of the writers use visual description: C, F.

One of the writers uses facts and statistics: C.

Page 61

(1)(2) e.g.

A. Both writers describe the natural world and express the great impact that it has on them.

D. In Text 1, the writer describes 'a deep, inexpressible awe that anything on this earth could be so vast, so beautiful, so silent.'

E. He repeats the word 'so' and uses a series of adjectives to highlight how powerful and impressive he finds the Grand Canyon.

C. The writer of Text 2 does not describe her reaction so clearly or in as much detail as the writer of Text 1.

H. She sums up her amazement by saying that the lights made her swear.

I. This suggests she cannot explain in words the effect that the lights have on her, which makes them seem all the more amazing.

Page 62

(1)

Identifies a similarity or difference in the two writers' ideas and perspectives.	Both writers try to describe the experience of seeing an amazing natural phenomenon: the Grand Canyon In Text 1 and the Northern Lights in Text 2.
Supports with a quotation or textual reference from Text 1.	The writer of Text 1 compares the 300 foot wide Colorado River to 'an old shoelace' as you look down on it from the top of the Grand Canyon.
Analyses the impact of the quotation from Text 1.	This comparison emphasises how massive and amazing the Canyon is.
Supports with a quotation or textual reference from Text 2.	The writer of Text 2 compares the Northern Lights to 'the eerie glow of a floodlit stadium or a picnic eaten in car headlights'.
Analyses the impact of the quotation from Text 2.	This shows how strange and unnatural the light of the Northern Lights is.
Compares how the two writers have conveyed their ideas and perspectives and/or compares the impact of the writers' choices on the reader.	Both writers use familiar, everyday objects and experiences to help the reader visualise unfamiliar and incredible wonders of the natural world.

(b) The student could develop their analysis of the writers' choices more fully, e.g. the choice of 'old' in Text 1 to belittle the scale of the river in comparison with the canyon; the choice of the comparison 'a picnic eaten in car headlights' which, as a strange and unusual way to eat a picnic, conveys the strangeness of the Northern Lights.

Page 64

Q	Text 2: *I Know Why The Caged Bird Sings* and Text 3: *A Back Seat Education* Compare how the writers of Text 2 and Text 3 present their ideas and perspectives about young people. Support your answer with detailed reference to the texts.　　　　　　　　(14 marks)
A	Both writers are sympathetic to young people. In Text 2, the narrator fears for her brother and the consequences of his actions; in Text 3, the writer remembers relationships on her school bus as 'exhausting' but she also remembers 'friendships so intense they burned'. Both writers present the world of young people as very different to the world of adults. In Text 2, the narrator tries to protect her brother from the adults' punishments; in Text 3, the writer remembers that, 'There were adults, of course, but they ignored us.' While the writer of Text 2 shows a young person in danger – both from the 'tigers and rippers' and from adult punishment – the writer of Text 3 presents young people as independent and happy: 'a tiny satisfied smile'.

Unit 9

Page 67

(1) (a) e.g. frightened, nervous

(b) 'anxious' and 'alarmed' are arguably the most precise and formal choices given.

(2) e.g. In the command to 'Look at me', and the question that follows, the writer <u>creates the impression</u> that Miss Havisham is <u>both</u> <u>domineering</u> <u>and</u> <u>disturbing</u>.

(3) e.g. wealthy, elderly, dishevelled, eccentric, unsettling.

Page 68

(1) C is arguably the most fluently, and sophisticatedly, expressed.

(2) e.g.

(a) The narrator suggests Miss Havisham is dying and decaying <u>when</u> he describes her as 'withered.'

(b) Pip is completely silent <u>until</u> he answers Miss Havisham's questions at the end of the extract.

(c) Pip is obviously terrified of Miss Havisham <u>because</u> he compares her to a waxwork and a skeleton.

Page 69

1. build/building; wear/wearing; sit/sitting; hide/hiding.

2. The narrator gives a long description of Miss Havisham's strange appearance, <u>building</u> up to the short, dramatic sentence, 'I should have cried out, if I could.'

3. **Note** that these non-finite clauses, using present participles, are moveable within the sentence, e.g.

   The image of Miss Havisham, wearing a faded wedding dress, sitting in her candle-lit dressing room and hiding from the outside world, is of a faded, almost decaying woman.

   OR

   The image of Miss Havisham, wearing a faded wedding dress and sitting in her candle-lit dressing room is of a faded, almost decaying woman, hiding from the outside world.

Page 70

1. e.g.

The narrator's description <u>creates</u> a <u>powerful impression</u> of the fear he <u>feels</u> for Miss Havisham <u>when</u> he describes her as a waxwork and a skeleton 'with dark eyes that moved and looked at me.' This is an <u>extremely</u> <u>disturbing</u> image. It suggests she is <u>decaying</u> and not human <u>and, as</u> she watches him carefully, creates the feeling that he is in danger.

076975   428GRA

Published by Pearson Education Limited, 80 Strand, London, WC2R ORL.

www.pearsonschoolsandfecolleges.co.uk

Text © Pearson Education Limited 2016
Produced and typeset by Tech-Set Ltd, Gateshead
Original illustrations © Pearson Education Ltd 2016

The right of David Grant to be identified as author of this work has been asserted by him in accordance with the Copyright, Designs and Patents Act 1988.

First published 2016

19 18 17
10 9 8 7 6 5 4 3 2

British Library Cataloguing in Publication Data
A catalogue record for this book is available from the British Library

ISBN 978 0435 18326 4

Printed in Slovakia by Neografia

Acknowledgements

We are grateful to the following for permission to reproduce copyright material:

Extract on page 18 from *Cider with Rosie* by Laurie Lee, Published by Chatto & Windus, Reprinted by permission of The Random House Group Limited; Extract on page 26 adapted from Fleet Street fox by Andrea Annear, *The Daily Mirror*, 2015, Reproduced with permission; Extract on page 34 adapted from How to survive the exam season by Nell Frizzell, *The Guardian*, 05/05/2015, Copyright © Guardian News & Media Ltd.; Extract on page 50 *Unreliable Memoirs* by Clive James, pub. Picador, London © Clive James 2008, with permission from Macmillan and Copyright © 2009, 1980 by Clive James. Used by permission of W. W. Norton & Company, Inc.; Extract on page 50 from *Where Memories Go* by Sally Magnusson, Hodder, 2014, Copyright © 2014 Sally Magnusson. Reproduced by permission of Hodder and Stoughton Limited; Extract on page 58 from *The Lost Continent* by Bill Bryson, Published by Transworld, Reprinted by permission of The Random House Group Limited and Brief excerpts from pp. 235, 237 from *The Lost Continent: Travels in Small-Town America* by Bill Bryson. Copyright © 1989 by Bill Bryson. Reprinted by permission of HarperCollins Publishers and Copyright © 1989 Bill Bryson. Reprinted by permission of Doubleday Canada, a division of Penguin Random House Canada Limited Extract on page 58 from *The Outrun* by Amy Liptrot, Canongate, 2016, Reproduced with permission; Extract on page 74 from *I Know Why the Caged Bird Sings* by Maya Angelou, Virago, 1969, Reproduced with permission from the Little, Brown Book Group Ltd.; Extract on page 75 from *A Back Seat Education* by Marianne Levy, *The Independent*, 16/01/2016, Reproduced with permission.